Confessions of an

AMATEUR BELIEVER

PATTY KIRK

OLIVER
NELSON

NELSON BOOKS
A Division of Thomas Nelson Publishers
Since 1798

www.thomasnelson.com

An entry into faith is a very private experience, comprising the most intimate details of a life, and, as a result, this is a very personal book. In it, I mention events and circumstances that many would not want even someone they loved to bring up in public. In some cases, I have changed names and blurred details or left them out entirely to make events less recognizable. But with my family such concealment was not possible. Some of them—especially my husband, my mother-in-law, and young daughters—have permitted their lives to be exposed through my ramblings, and for this I am especially grateful.

Published in Nashville, Tennessee, by Thomas Nelson, Inc.

Nelson Books titles may be purchased in bulk for educational, business, fund-raising, or sales promotional use. For information, please e-mail SpecialMarkets@ThomasNelson.com.

Unless otherwise noted, Scripture quotations are taken from the HOLY BIBLE, NEW INTERNATIONAL VERSION®. Copyright © 1973, 1978, 1984 by International Bible Society. Used by permission of Zondervan Bible Publishing House. All rights reserved.

The "NIV" and "New International Version" trademarks are registered in the United States Patent and Trademark Office by International Bible Society. Use of either trademark requires the permission of International Bible Society.

Scripture quotations noted KJV are from The Holy Bible, KING JAMES VERSION.

Scripture quotations noted CEV are from THE CONTEMPORARY ENGLISH VERSION of the Bible. Copyright © 1991,1995 by the American Bible Society. Used by permission.

Scripture quotations noted RSV are from the REVISED STANDARD VERSION of the Bible. Copyright © 1946, 1952, 1971, 1973 by the Division of Christian Education of the National Council of the Churches of Christ in the U.S.A. Used by permission.

Scriptures marked ESV are from The Holy Bible, ENGLISH STANDARD VERSION. Copyright © 2001 by Crossway Bibles, a division of Good News Publishers.

Library of Congress Cataloging-in-Publication Data

Kirk, Patty.
    Confessions of an amateur believer / Patty Kirk.
        p. cm.
    ISBN 10: 0-7852-2041-0 (pbk.)
    ISBN 13: 978-0-7852-2041-1
    1. Christian converts—Biography. 2. Conversion—Christianity—Biography.
I. Title.
BV4936.K49A3 2006
277.3'082092—dc22
                                                2006006609

Printed in the United States of America

1 2 3 4 5 6 RRD 09 08 07 06

Words of Praise for *Confessions of an Amateur Believer*

Kirk's thoughts on concepts such as servanthood, intercessory prayer, fairness and priorities glitter with humor and honesty. On a deeper level, her ruminations shine with a heart-deep knowledge that God understands her struggles, and that her trials are made easier by knowing him. This is a lovely book both for Kirk's fine writing and for her search for God that encompasses all readers. "If, in the darkness, I stop worrying to listen—which I often don't, or can't, or won't—I hear God's voice under the narrative of my own worries and accusations: That's enough.

—Publishers Weekly

With quick wit and unflagging honesty, Patty Kirk traces her journey from simple childhood faith, through an unwilling atheism, to a rediscovery of Christian belief. Her meditations on the difficulties of faith ring true and never stoop to sentimentalism. She resembles a gentle Anne Lamott in her self-deprecating humor, entertaining tales of her children and daily life, and abiding faith amid struggle.

—Susan VanZanten Gallagher
Professor of English, Seattle Pacific University
Director, Center for Scholarship and Faculty Development

Spiritual autobiography can so easily degenerate into sentimentality or subtle egotism, but Patty Kirk's *Confessions of an Amateur Believer* does neither. Her varied reflections—from cows to critical thinking—are by turns wry, humorous and touched with wonder. . . .

—Mary Stewart van Leeuwen
Professor of psychology and philosophy at Eastern College
in St. Davids, Pennsylvania, and resident scholar
at its Center for Christian Women in Leadership

The book is a progression, of a life—of pain, anguish, understanding, acceptance, and delight. Each phase is a confession. In the end there are passages of deep understanding of life and, well, theology.

—Hyatt Moore
Former President of Wycliffe Bible Translators USA

Patty Kirk's quiet memoir walks through the loss of glimmering faith to a recovery rooted in intellectual honesty and attentiveness to day-to-day experience. Hers is the sort of book that will motivate readers to regard the meaning of their own daily lives, a service to all of us.

—DALE BROWN
Professor of English, Director, Emeritus, Festival of Faith & Writing

It is so very encouraging to read what I myself have felt so many times. Thanks for having the courage to reveal so much of yourself thereby making the Christian journey real. I know that your book will be helpful to all who read it.

—LINDA MOON
Global Teams missionary, Regional Mobilization
Coordinator, Birmingham, AL

Patty Kirk's book will surprise readers who think that *Jesus Camp* is a reliable guide to "evangelical Christianity." She shatters preconceptions right and left, simply by telling the story of how she came to faith and how she lives each day as an "amateur believer."

—JOHN WILSON
Editor, *Books & Culture*

Kirk's reflections are insightful, sometimes showing her poetic creativity and at other times showing her academic leanings but at all times revealing her straightforwardness . . . I felt that I was reading a private diary offering insights to which I should not be privy. On reflection, this shows Kirk's desire to be totally transparent to the reader. She wants people to know of her deeply personal wrestling with faith which she connects to the cosmic battle evidenced in Martin Luther surrendering to God. This book is therefore a deeply personal lens into the movement into faith, a journey that portrays most aspects of a woman who is a mother and a wife and a true believer.

—REV. HOWARD WORSLEY
Director of Education, Church of England, Schools,
Youth and Children's Ministries
Diocese of Southwell and Nottingham

To the many believers who knowingly and unknowingly nourished my spirit from my earliest childhood through years of atheism and back to faith. Also to my students and colleagues at John Brown University, to my sweet husband Kris, who supports me in everything, and especially to my daughters, Charlotte and Lulu, who challenge my faith daily and help me sustain it.

Contents

Introduction

Often, when people speak about their faith, they describe it as a settled thing. A thing acquired, sometimes on a certain date, and utterly static. Not merely "once saved, always saved," as my husband liked to hope when he met me as an atheist who had once believed, but "once saved, always the same," having the same exact faith as what they started out with their entire lives. Part of me envies that sort of certainty. Such faith journeys from conversion to death, as I envision them, follow a clean, sure trajectory reminiscent of the lives and deaths of Catholic martyrs in a book I had as a child. Never faltering in the faith. Never questioning. Always obedient. Their eyes cast ever skyward in the woodcut illustrations that accompanied the text.

Other faithful men and women of scripture, though, seem just the opposite. Peter. John the Baptist in prison, about to be beheaded. Mary and Martha when their brother dies. Jesus' own mother, who experienced his divine heritage firsthand and called on him for miracles, but at the height of his ministry went with his brothers "to take charge of him, for they said, 'He is out of his mind'" (Mark 3:21). Most heroes of faith, it seems to me, spend as much time wandering away from God as they do returning to him. And many great believers balk at the crucial moment, often late in their lives, when one would think their faith as mature and large as it will ever be. Theirs is a jagged faith trajectory at best. Like Jacob—like me—they must wrestle with God and with themselves for a long time before they can receive their blessing.

I have met people who have told me that they became believers in childhood, and I have always thought, *Who doesn't believe in God in childhood?* In the force that created green and water and dogs and sunlight? In those invisible qualities of love, justice, order, and forgiveness? Arms to run to when we are hurt. The confidence that we are right, or wrong, in our actions. The daily rituals of getting up and being fed and napping and playing and going to bed again. Being heard and paid attention to. Being loved, no matter what.

Ideally, we see glimpses of God's essential qualities in our parents and in the life they provide for us. But even in the absence of these natural sources of nurture—if you will allow me to indulge one of my deepest hopes about who God is—even the most neglected and abused of children see God, if only in increments of time too fleeting for those around them to acknowledge, in the love acts of some kind friend or acquaintance. God's invisible presence is unmistakable—it must be—in the bleakest of settings, if our senses are motivated, as the senses of children are, by dependence and need.

Unbelief comes later. Beset by troubles, or else blinded to our fundamental need and dependence by ease and by our increasing ability to take care of ourselves, some of us lose sight of God. Or we forget to look for him. As we do when a loved one dies, we eventually become accustomed to days and nights without the one we loved and gradually forget the contours of a face we once knew with our eyes closed. Soon, mourning itself is a distant memory, replaced by the more urgent activities of daily life. As time passes, we struggle to remember the person at all and carry with us only a vague sense of loss.

That is unbelief, I think. The nagging absence of a remembered face. Sometimes a certain smell or touch or sound we associate with the one we have lost reminds us. Sometimes, in the night, we dream the person live and real again. But, our practical selves wake us up and convince us of what seems, in loss, to be the only reality: we are alone. Unbelief, in my experience, is much less a conscious rejection of God than a sense of abandonment and loss. A sense of our own aloneness. And the certainty that no effort on our part can restore to us the one we loved. The prayer of the unbeliever—Lord, help my unbelief!—is the voice of hope from beneath our loneliness and self-made comforts. It is the seed out of which true faith grows.

But the faith of many of our spiritual heroes—Moses, Jonah, Mary, Peter—does not always arc upward from that first moment of belief to godliness. Often, we progress only to fall back, and our biggest spiritual steps "higher up and deeper in," in the words of C. S. Lewis, are often out of pits into which we have fallen, again and again, along the way. That's progress. Falling back into moments of unbelief to rediscover God, then picking oneself up and proceeding forward, ever forward to the safety of his fatherly arms and into the genuine rest he promises his beloved children.

This book explores how, having begun to believe as a child and lost sight of God for half a lifetime, I came not only to recognize him again but, by struggling with scripture and my own habits of unbelief, to acknowledge and celebrate his active participation in my life.

The first section, "Meeting God," follows my initial journey out of unbelief into faith. I came to that first encounter with a history that played a crucial role in my ultimate ability to recognize God's authority and power. My struggle, however, had only just begun, and the chapters in the second section, "Struggling," describe my ensuing faith wrestling. In the third section, "Progress," the wrestling continues, but in these chapters I experiment with my new habits of trusting in the one who comes to explain everything to us and finding answers to many lifelong questions. The chapters in the final section, "Rest," explore the most essential gifts of God: an end to the striving and sweating and questioning that have been our lot since the fall. We will drink milk and wine we didn't have to go to the store to buy. We will love one another, perfectly, in spite of ourselves. We will truly and totally enjoy pursuing God's will over our own. We will rest.

Meeting God

1

The Faith of a Child

Unlike most of the people I go to church with these days, I wasn't always much of a believer. Although as a child I attended church weekly and did believe in God, I never heard of concepts like having a "personal relationship" with Christ or just giving my troubles to Jesus. My relationship with Jesus Christ was, at best, respectful but remote, like my relationships with relatives I knew only from my parents' stories. As I was growing up, my troubles took me not into the arms of God but ever further from the faith of my childhood, and I spent a big part of my adult life unable to believe at all.

I grew up one of six kids in a Catholic family. I was baptized not long after I was born, and we attended church every Sunday, where I listened to three readings from the Bible weekly: one from Psalms, one from the Epistles, and one from the Gospels. I made my first communion when I was six or seven. At twelve I was confirmed in my faith by reciting my baptismal vows and adding the name of a saint to my other names.

Polycarp. I had to fight the nuns and get permission from our

Monsignor to use a male name. I chose Polycarp, I explained to Msgr. Dziodosz, not just because his feast day was my birthday but because I liked his story in our family's *Little Pictorial Lives of Saints*. Faced with martyrdom unless he cursed Christ, Polycarp replied, "Eighty-six years I have served Him, and He never did me wrong; how can I blaspheme my King and Saviour?" In my child's mind, Polycarp was saying, "Well, I've followed God for so long that it hardly seems worthwhile to change now." The strange pragmatism of this statement of faith struck me as funny.

My family ate fish sticks on Fridays when I was young, and we carried in our station wagon a cross-shaped wooden box that twisted open to reveal a bottle of holy water, a white silk stole, and a rolled up sheet of paper with instructions on how to perform an emergency baptism. Sometimes, when my parents drove us places, I fantasized about coming upon an accident and watching my father crouch beside a dying person to read the words on the paper, getting spots of blood on the stole.

This was in the sixties, before the modernizations of the Second Vatican Council had really sunk in. In those days, my sisters and I wore organdy dresses poufed out with stiff slips to church and lace caps bobby-pinned to the tops of our heads. My older sister Sharon told funny stories about the nuns at a parochial school she had attended for awhile when I was just little. I coveted a soft focus painting of Jesus praying that night on Gethsemane that Sharon had above her bed—the sky the inkiest midnight blue above what I thought of as the cheery lights of Bethlehem twinkling below.

My dad told stories, too. Of stealing the communion wine in his altar boy days. Of a gigantic nun who punished him by lifting him off the ground by that especially tender hair that grows at the temple. Of his uncles shouting, "Jaysus, Mary, and Joseph." Of snow and knickerbockers and growing up in Brooklyn, which were all part of my Catholic heritage, as it seemed to me.

On Christmas Eve some years, my parents took us to midnight Mass. Imagine it. You're six or seven or eight years old and have never stayed up past nine o'clock, not for any reason, and certainly not on Christmas Eve, that night of nights when presents appear out of nowhere and the air itself quivers with carols. You were so excited when they put you to bed that you couldn't sleep for a long time, but now, seconds later it seems, your parents get you and your siblings up out of the warm covers and thrust you into your church clothes. Nobody talks much. It is the middle of the middle of the night, and the world is darker and quieter than it has ever been in your remembrance. And then you're riding in the back of the station wagon, and then you're in the cold church, waiting.

Your mother or father gives your siblings and you each a little candle from a box at the end of the pew. It has a paper apron around it that your mother whispers is there to protect your hand from drips of wax. And then the lights go out, and the whole church is dark except for a leafy crèche at the altar: a Hawaiian-looking house surrounded by palm fronds. And you sit in the dark, waiting.

Soon there is a shuffling noise from behind, and you crane around to see. First, some altar boys appear, some of them only your age or younger, carrying gigantic candles on poles. Then, behind them, the priests, swinging censors wafting the exotic smoke of frankincense and myrrh. It is a fabulous smell that collects in your nose and sinks to your lowest places and stays there. Days later your closet will smell of that night.

The priests wear white vestments and Christmas-colored stoles, and the Monsignor has on his magenta hat with the pompom, and they all look old fashioned, somehow, like Santa Clauses from an ancient book. Then your father or your mother lights your candle and your sisters' and brothers' candles, and then the whole church is filled with the glow and smell of candles burning, and everyone sits in the unfamiliar light and the silence and waits. Finally, the priest starts the mass, and you sing carols, and everyone files past the crèche for communion.

At that time, I knew this about God: He was real. Although he lived in heaven, he was everywhere too. He knew me and heard me and could see me every moment of the day. He could see into my very thoughts. He had a son who was born in a Hawaiian-looking house surrounded by farm animals and shepherds and his mother and father. The son was real, too. Even though he was later killed on a cross, he came alive again and then went to heaven, where he still is, and he knew me just as his father did. And because of this, the ghost of him lived in me, and someday I would die and go to heaven where God and Jesus were and live there with them forever.

My faith as a child was, in other words, not much different from my evangelical Christian faith now. I believed in God and in his son, in his son's death and resurrection, and in my own resulting salvation from death. I wasn't very clear on the idea of sin, it's true, but I knew God loved me enough to forgive me and others for whatever we did wrong. I believed in the Father, the Son, and the Holy Spirit. I believed in eternal life.

In the intervening years, as an atheist, I married a Christian, and he told me that this faith of my Catholic childhood was enough for him, even though I had abandoned it—or, as I felt, it had abandoned me. My childhood faith was enough, in fact, for God himself, this silly little man who married me told me. "Once saved, always saved," he said—which, he explained to me, meant

6

it wasn't possible to lose true faith in God. It was a new concept for me. But I knew he was wrong. The faint glimmer of the faith I had once had was not enough to fill me with the light of genuine belief. That much I knew. And without faith, I was not saved. I was not a Catholic. Not a Christian. Not going to heaven or anywhere else when I died, no matter what anyone told me. And there was nothing I could do about it.

Faith, I somehow intuited, must come from outside of me. It must come from God himself, if it was true at all. And it didn't come, so it must not be true. That was my atheism.

Now, though, looking back, I wonder if my husband was right. Perhaps, even as a child, I did believe enough to be clutched back to the bosom of God had I lain me down to sleep one night and died. Perhaps, if I had died some more realistic death—from a disease like the one that killed my mother or in an accident—perhaps even in those later years when I no longer felt loved or heard or even noticed by God, when my prayers disappeared into the black vacuum of night and I knew no one was listening, perhaps even then I would have survived death because of the almost forgotten faith of my childhood.

But for years, my husband's trite assurance that I believed, no matter what I thought, amused me. I knew what I knew. Or what I didn't know. And even years later, when I became a believer again, it seemed to be not from sin that I was saved but from that black night of my inability to believe. Not from hell and death but from the conviction that, contrary to what I believed as a child, I was *not* seen and known and heard when I prayed, I was *not* loved by God.

My years of atheism have made such an impression on me—the hope I hid from my friends, the longing for something beyond what I saw around me, my complete inability to pray—that I often forget about the faith of my childhood. And it may be merely a vestige of that child's worldview, made up of presents and nighttime ceremonies and the familiar Christmas decorations we took out of dusty boxes every year and arranged on the mantle, but the crux of Christianity for me has never been the cross. Not then, not now. Instead, it is God's first response to our hope and longing and frustrating blindness: the birth of his own son in our world. What matters most to me is that God *had* that son to begin with. And that he has other sons and daughters like me that he loves and doesn't want to be parted from. That he loves his children as I love my own daughters, only more so, with a hot, knowing, parental love that says, "Be who you are, but love me back. Only love me back."

I wear a certain necklace a lot, a silver baby on a chain. People I know at school and church and sometimes even strangers come up to me and ask me what it means.

"Are you showing that you're against abortion?" they ask me.

So I explain that no, it's not an aborted baby but a baby Jesus. I prefer wearing the baby Jesus to wearing a cross, I tell them.

If it's around Christmastime, they usually nod approvingly, but if it's Easter-time, I usually have to say a bit more. Actually, the baby is really a Mardi Gras king-cake baby that I bought in New Orleans, a detail which could complicate my explanation somewhat because of the natural association of Mardi Gras with Lent and thus Easter, but I don't ever try to explain any of that.

Sometimes I consider this exchange an important opportunity to correct the macabre habit my fellow evangelicals have of bringing the crucifixion into every discussion of who God is, even discussions of the birth of Jesus. At my church's Christmas sing-along, someone invariably requests "Up from the Grave He Arose" or "I Am Redeemed by the Blood of the Lamb!" Wearing a baby on a chain is my attempt to get them see the ghoulishness of such thinking.

But the bigger ministry of my little necklace is to myself. Hanging from that chain is not the baby Jesus at all but me, one of God's daughters. A cherished daughter who once knew him a long time ago and, without thinking about it much, simply loved him back, as children do. A wayward daughter to whom he revealed himself almost from her birth but who nevertheless ran from him and refused to love him back, despite the almost constant evidences of his enduring love and protection. I am, mysteriously, God's own baby girl. One of many children whom the Father sent his Son into our burning world to carry home to him.

One year during midnight Mass, when the dark was suddenly lit up with candles and we were waiting in the blaze for the mass to begin, my baby brother Tim yelled into the holy silence, "And now everybody sing 'Happy Birthday' to me!!"

The silence deepened for a second or two with my family's embarrassment, then Msgr. Dziodosz boomed from the altar his deep laughter. Exactly like Santa Claus. And then everyone else laughed too.

Relevant and cited scriptural passages: Luke 2:1–20.
Other references:
John Gilmary Shea. *Little Pictorial Lives of Saints*. 1878.

2

Empty Spaces in the Ash

As a child, I was fascinated by Pompeii. We had a unit in one of our schoolbooks about Roman civilization and the eruption of Mount Vesuvius. Like most kids, we adored volcanoes, but Vesuvius was especially exciting because of the casts of its burnt up victims that archaeologists had made by pouring plaster into the empty spaces their bodies had left behind in the hardened ash.

Our teacher showed us shiny black and white photographs of the plaster casts. Fire informed every gesture, every bend of a joint. There were men and women who appeared to be crawling or unconscious. Children screaming, their mouths yawning in agony. A dog in a strangely beautiful twisted curve, head to feet. Unless it is some trick of memory, or that innate urge I often have to tell a story bigger than it really is, our teacher even drew our attention to their "natural poses," as if such statuary from a real life disaster could be anything but natural.

The Pompeiians, we learned, had running water and elaborate baths, ornate with artwork. Close-ups of these household murals and mosaics told the story of what everyday life in the city was like before Vesuvius erupted. Surprisingly contemporary looking people sat in meetings, walked their dogs, bathed, ate meals, tilled the soil, made love, danced. In the mosaics, their faces and bodies were flat and fragmented. Missing tiles were filled in with plaster. The mosaics looked nothing like the plaster casts, and I struggled to reconcile these two versions of the people of Pompeii in my mind. Which was more true to life, I wondered, the fragmentary scenes from their actual lives, or plaster that had taken the shape of the emptiness their dying bodies had left behind?

It was hard for me to imagine why the mosaics existed in the first place. I tried to envision my family's tiled bathroom representing scenes from *our* everyday life. My mom coming home from the grocery store in our beat-up, blue station wagon. My sisters and brothers and me eating our afternoon snack of Monterey Jack cheese and apricot nectar on the patio out back. Us all going to church. My dad sitting behind his desk at work, a scene I had never seen and could only reconstruct in my mind from his spare dinner table comments about his day and the perfect little numbers he penciled in the center of each green square of the graph paper he used to figure on. I imagined our tiled faces, broken, by the limitations of the art form as well as by time and devastation, into strange little isolations of color and texture. Close up, our faces would be unrecognizable as anything but twisted grids filled with glaze. In another space in my mind, I couldn't imagine this bathroom at all.

Years later, I saw a pieced quilt like those mosaics: an enormous picture, made out of tiny scraps of dun-colored fabric, of the face of Jesus, wearing his crown of thorns. I can't remember exactly when and where I saw it—maybe on the stage in the auditorium of the Catholic high school I attended for a couple of years when we lived in Connecticut, maybe at an ecumenical conference in the Anaheim Convention Center that I went to as a teen sometime after we moved back to California, maybe behind the altar of some big church I visited in Europe or China as a wandering young adult. The woman who had made the quilt spread it out first in some cramped space—between the front row of seats and a stage or kneeling rail, I think—for us to look at, but not to touch or walk on. It was too big for the space, and she had to keep bunching some parts together and pulling folds open so we could see what she told us were parts of Jesus' face: the mouth, the eyes, the crown, the hair.

"See?" she asked us, and we peered into the cloth between her hands, seeing nothing. Close up, each part was brown and indistinguishable from the rest, just rags torn from old clothes she had bought by the pound from Salvation Armies everywhere she went. Some of the seams were backwards, exposed, and she hadn't even taken the trouble to snip the thread at the ends of them, and I remember thinking the quilt ill made. I was into sewing, esteeming a tidy hem, a neatly finished seam.

Then the artist got some men, and they dragged the heavy quilt between them up to some hooks on cables hanging from a high ceiling and winched it up. The face became clear to us as the quilt inched upward. We backed up to see it better. It was amazing how real looking the assembled rags became, how the yellowed fabric and torn edges and threads became skin and anguish. I heard the people around me wondering over it, murmuring my thoughts: "How did she know how to do it? Could she see the whole picture as she pieced the individual scraps? She must have worked from a sketch—don't you think?—and just filled in between the lines with different hues, like a gigantic paint by numbers."

Viewed thus from afar, it was a face I recognized from childhood, one I knew and believed in—in the same half-conscious sense that I knew and believed in other things as far back as I could remember. I believed in love, that my parents loved me and each other, that we always would love each other. I believed in gravity, that an apple, dropped, would fall to the ground. I believed in these things, but their importance didn't really grip me. So I loved my parents, so there was a God, so apples fell. So what?

Sometime after that I lost even that much belief in God. Things had gone steadily downhill in my family. The move to Connecticut, my parents decided, had been a mistake. The winters were too hard. We lived on a country road that the snowplow didn't clear. Renovating the beautiful colonial house we had bought—built in 1770—was harder work than my parents could manage in addition to my dad's job in far-off Hartford and my mom's more than full-time job of raising the six of us. They labored to expose the hand-hewn chestnut beams buried beneath layer upon layer of modernization. I remember coming home from school to find my mother hacking at the living room walls or ceiling or Zip-Stripping the split-plank floors upstairs. She usually wore a mask of some sort, a scarf or a rag tied tight around the lower part of her face, and all you could see were her eyes, tired and mad and desperate looking, below her permed hair, invariably matted with plaster dust or stripper gunk or little pink shreds of fiberglass insulation. My poor mom. Paintbrush in hand, she gave me and my sisters muffled instructions about what to fix for dinner or which rooms needed scrubbed or vacuumed. Despite all the rubble of renovation, the house still had to stay clean.

My mom started acting kind of crazy even before we moved back to California. She cried a lot and got lost driving. She constantly threatened to leave my dad and us, I found out much later.

Once, when we were going Christmas shopping in Hartford, she just kept getting off the highway at the same wrong exit to the mall. We looped around again and again until finally she gave up, shrieking at our disappointment. She was always screaming at us, and we hated her. My older sister Sharon ran away from home to escape her. My next younger sister Joanie and I started hanging out with the bad kids at school. Our younger siblings fought all the time. My dad was a mess.

Not long after we got to California, my mom was diagnosed with a grapefruit-sized brain tumor and operated on the next day. Against all odds, she survived the operation and spent the next eleven years slowly dying. During that time, my parents divorced, my dad remarried, and my mom moved in with my sister Sharon.

Our mother was not easy to look after. For one thing, she would not stay put. After the operation, she was blind but for a little pinpoint of light in one eye. Nevertheless, we had to forcibly remove her car keys and license to keep her from screeching around the neighborhood in one of our big, boat-like cars. Carless, she escaped on foot—to the grocery store, on buses to who knows where, around town. In the supermarkets she was known to fill her cart up with so much old bread and dented cans and pickled beets on special that she could no longer push it. She always liked a bargain.

She lost her sense of balance and fell a lot. She also had seizures from time to time. She had no short-term memory. Several times she overdosed on her various medicines because she forgot that she had already taken them.

Sharon had to quit her job just to keep her at home and safe. At home, as the brain-impaired often do, my mom became paranoid. She accused Sharon's boyfriend Tom of stealing things—her purse, her Bible, the bacon. How Sharon managed in that wild time to be wooed and wed, I will never know. She also became what she called a "born-again Christian."

I was living abroad by then, first in Germany, then China, then Hong Kong, as far away from my unhappy family as I could get. My occasional flights home to see my mom—one last time before she dies, I always thought—were punctuated by vehement fights with Sharon about God. And there would sit my mom, slightly askew and smiling crazily, at the kitchen table. She was mostly bald from radiation therapy, but, out of some lingering vanity, she wouldn't let anyone cut her remaining wisps of graying hair, and they stuck out like dark flames around her head.

I cannot pin down one certain event or period in all of this that caused me to lose all sense I had of there even being a God, much less one who loved and took care of us. Neither my mom's illness nor subsequent death, not my parents' divorce, not my travels in other countries. But somewhere in the topsy-turvy murk of my late teens and early twenties, I stopped believing in everything. Love, God, gravity, the whole shebang.

It was my loss of belief in God that bothered me the most, though. When I tried to explain it to anyone, I couldn't. It was just, like, not there anymore. I didn't know who had created me, and I sure didn't know why. I was just there. And someday I wouldn't be. I thought back with longing to a time when I knew the answers to things. I wanted desperately to believe there were answers. I wanted my thoughts and desires to stop flying apart, to fall back together, back to their right places, where I could recognize and know them. But it just wasn't possible. I couldn't get my faith back. I wasn't even sure if I had ever really had it.

I was sort of happy, though. My life was an entertaining series of boyfriends and languages and pleasantly lonely afternoons spent reading and baking cakes. I learned a lot. I earned just enough money teaching English to eat and rent an apartment and pay for plane tickets to somewhere new. I rarely saw my family but was on good terms with all of them.

Toward the end of her life, my mom went into a coma, and I was able to fly home and see her living body just before she died. She looked dead already. She lay in a curve on one side in a rented hospital bed in the guestroom at Sharon's house where I usually slept when I visited them. Her yellowish skin was baggy looking and rough. Her bones, inside the skin, seemed smaller than I remembered them—tiny and fragile and very apparent, like a newborn's bones. She smelled bad and made that terrible breathing noise of the dying. She did not look like my mother.

Right after my arrival, Sharon wanted me to help her turn my mom over on her other side to prevent bedsores. I didn't want to— in truth, I didn't want to touch her—but I agreed. I took her feet. They were spotted, contagious looking, sticking out from beneath her pink nylon nightgown. Her toes were horn-nailed and clenched against the pads of her feet. I tried not to look at them as I held her ankles in my hands, but looked instead at Sharon and waited for directions. Sharon was bent over the head of the bed, her whole arms under my mother's torso to bear the weight, her face upside-down against my mother's as if she were trying, at this late stage, to breathe life into her.

After we turned my mom, Sharon stayed bent over like that, stroking her and kissing her and talking to her softly, explaining, "There, that wasn't so bad. We just needed to turn you over so you won't hurt, just so you won't hurt." It was a strange childlike voice that spoke these words, a voice I remembered from some early,

early day in my life when I was hurt and my big sister became my mother for a moment and nursed me.

It's now years later. I have married, have had children of my own, and have come to believe—in a new way—in the God who made us in his image and mourned our inability to live up to it and sent his own son for us to kill so that we might be with him beyond our several deaths. Somehow, in the interim, God pieced that memory of my sister comforting our dying mother together with a thousand other frayed remnants of my life to make himself gradually recognizable to me again.

And although it was not then, at the foot of my mother's deathbed, but much later that my faith in love and gravity and God were restored to me, still my life did begin to settle then, and from time to time that irretrievable day still seizes me, and its images demand my notice. Those feet. That tiny ugly body, curved in near death to the pose of an infant in the womb. The screaming gasp for one last breath of air. My sister leaning over, speaking sweetly, willing our mother not to hurt, not to die. Here I find the what and why of existence. Loss and mourning. Suffering and love. God bending down to breathe life into us. Or to listen. Or softly speak.

What fascinated me most about those plaster casts from Pompeii was how they came to be made in the first place. I've always wanted to read an account of the person who made the first casts, preserving thus into eternity all those people in all that pain. How did anyone ever think of doing it, or find the gaps in the petrified ash where others' suffering, now long past, could be arrested in time and brought to our notice?

And what motivated the person to look in the first place? Mere curiosity? Some crass scientific need to see what dying looked like?

Or was it something better, higher? Pity, perhaps. The desire to know another's pain, to document and remember and mourn what was lost, and perhaps even redeem it for some future good.

Or perhaps, like that first filling of our clay forms with life in Genesis, the archaeologist was inspired by the sheer excitement of creation. To make something appear where before there was nothing but an empty space in the dirt. To pour in substance and meaning and reclaim the vacuum as an object of wonder. To look on it and find it good.

Relevant and cited scriptural passages: Genesis 1–2.

3

An Exodus

I grew up with a girl whose mom had done the most amazing thing. Actually, it was Melanie's grandparents who did it—her mom was only a child at the time, merely the recipient of her parents' action. Here it is: Melanie's Jewish grandparents, who owned a hotel in pre-War Berlin, sent Melanie's mom and her sister off to England to be raised by another family they didn't know while they themselves fled to Bolivia. They didn't see their daughters again until they were grown.

It wasn't a thing my friend Melanie or anyone else in her family talked about very often, and it wasn't until I was an adult living in Berlin myself and Melanie's mom returned to the city of her childhood for the first time that I really understood it in its entirety. I learned the story bit by bit throughout my childhood, shadowy fragments of narrative that fascinated and confused me, inextricably matted in with the equally fascinating and confusing story of who Melanie and her family were to begin with.

They were musical. Melanie's mom played viola da gamba and taught Suzuki violin. Her brother Geoffrey played violin and listened to the most terrifying hard rock records I had ever heard. Melanie herself played cello and piano and later, in the school band, tuba. They had a music room lined with shelves and cubbyholes full of stringed instruments and wooden recorders of all sizes. At Christmastime their musical friends would assemble, filling the music room and spilling into the muddy hallway and out the back door into the snow to play carols on the recorders. It was like being in a happy scene in a Dickens novel to hear them, to see their red faces and bright scarves and the sheet music fluttering in the wind.

Melanie's family ate anchovy paste and wrinkled Greek olives and tough, chewy bread, and they raised goats for milk and made their own cheese. They took me swimming at a quarry surrounded by DANGER! NO TRESPASSING! signs, where I was the only swimmer who wore a bathing suit. The family's cluttered colonial house was full of handmade objects and treasures from far-off lands—handloomed rugs and a real Modigliani drawing and tiny red beans full of even tinier ivory elephants.

Like houses in dreams, Melanie's house seemed to gain dusty attics and seductive, off-limits rooms every time I visited. The family attended a Quaker church that had "silent meetings," and they once smoked marijuana together to celebrate Easter. Their house was always full of people speaking different languages. Melanie had a German-speaking grandmother, whom she called Muni, and once traveled to Switzerland with her family and brought back a glass-enclosed edelweiss flower on a chain that I always coveted and a real eggshell, unbroken, filled with a nutty chocolate cream called nougat. Everything about Melanie and her family thrilled me.

I must have been ten or twelve—about the age when I read and reread *The Diary of Anne Frank* and *Robinson Crusoe*—when I learned that Melanie's mom's parents had sent her mom off across the ocean to be raised by strangers. I imagined the shadowy weeping parents pushing their dark-eyed daughters out of a heavy door into the rain. The logistics of how the two girls got from Berlin to England always perplexed me until Melanie explained, with the irritated voice she always had whenever I pressed her for details about her mom's amazing past, that they used the underground railroad. Like my own daughters when they studied the history of slavery, I thought this meant an actual railroad under the ground, a sort of subway beneath the war and the sea that the Nazis didn't know about, an escape as real and as terrifying as Anne Frank's Annex behind the bookshelf.

Only later did I read about the *Kindertransport* and the Quakers' other humanitarian efforts on behalf of Holocaust victims and figure out the connection between the underground railroad and the family's Quaker faith. And when Melanie's mom and dad stayed with me in Berlin years and years later, sleeping on a futon on the floor of my apartment and eating whey cheese and *doppelkrust* rye bread in my tiny kitchen, I finally connected the music and strange food and visits to psychoanalysts with the chopped-up life Melanie's mom had lived: the cultural center Berlin had been in the thirties, those lifesaving Quakers sneaking around, the daughters' confusion and fear on leaving their parents behind, the mysterious adoptive family in England. I finally understood what I sensed was Melanie's mom's fascination, but also hatred and terror, for the home she had left behind as a child and what had to have been her own parents' absolute despair that anything could ever be right in that place again.

Or was it despair, I wonder? Is it hope or hopelessness that leads one to send one's child to a place of safety?

I have always had a fascination with refugees. I cry listening to interviews from refugee camps on National Public Radio. That strange combination of hope and despair in their voices, the descriptions of what they carry with them and what they leave behind—I hear my own mind's dark voice in their vain attempts to explain their situation to this stranger with the microphone from a country where there is no war or disease or even real hunger.

I was a refugee myself. I can't say I fled an oppressive government, but I went to city after city—first in the U.S., then in Europe and Asia—to escape, I've lately come to realize, the aftermath of a crime that was at once so arbitrary and contrived that it left me in a kind of hopelessness about my world that I have never entirely recovered from.

As a graduate student in New Orleans, I was held up at gunpoint in a phone booth at night, sexually assaulted, robbed of what few personal belongings I had with me as well as my students' and my end-of-term papers, and then subjected to the police officers' trivialization of what had happened to me, my students' rage over the lost papers and grade book, my professors' disbelief, and my own self-blame.

Like the story of Melanie's mom, my story reads like some shadowy fairy tale from another time, not really my own life. Whenever I tell it, I feel as if I have jumbled the details, or made them up entirely. One thing about it is clear to me now, though. After it happened, I left. I packed up a few key belongings—certain outfits that traveled well that I wore so often they were like uniforms, an address book with a picture of a mummy glued on the front of it, a few old ceramic bowls and some paintings done by friends that I could not leave behind, a white enamel pot in which I could cook anything—and I left that place. I did not look back.

I left again and again, whenever my life got chaotic or scary. Whenever relationships went awry or I was bored with life or I found myself enraged at a stranger riding the subway. I simply left wherever I was and started over somewhere else, preferably somewhere I had never been before, with an entirely different language, where I knew no one.

It was that easy, that hard. In retrospect, I feel I don't know the person who did it. The person who packed bags, paid for flights, matriculated at foreign universities, found jobs and new friends and places to stay on little money. If things got that bad again now, I wonder, could I do the same thing all over again? If my house were bombed, if my children were threatened or hungry, would I be able to pack up what I could carry and just leave?

That was the part of the Elián Gonzalez story that intrigued me most. You remember that Cuban woman who set off for Florida in a boat with her five-year-old son and drowned before she got there, leaving him clinging to a rubber inner tube? I wonder, could I do that? To escape Cuba, my home, however miserable or terrified I was there, could I, like Elián Gonzalez's poor mom, get in a row boat and take on the ocean? Could I, like Melanie's Omi, send my precious girls off to another country, alone, away from me, even to save their lives? I try to imagine myself in a boat fleeing with my daughters, Charlotte and Lulu, back when they were Elián's age. I am trying to row against unpredictable waves; they are climbing me in their terror, screaming, pinioning my arms, suffocating me.

After wandering the world for years, I found myself in a bar on an island near Hong Kong where I was living, staring at the expatriates who were my friends at the time. The Scottish bartender regularly threw himself from the ferry in an attempt to commit suicide. His Brazilian wife had killed herself the year before with an overdose of sleeping pills. A British neighbor of mine was in love with a local girl, who was engaged to be married to someone else and screamed "I hate you! I hate you! I hate you!" over and over again from behind the mosquito netting shrouding my neighbor's bed. An emphysemic man of indeterminate age was hacking his lungs out in a corner of the bar, telling some story in his hoary voice to whoever would listen. Among those not listening was a middle-aged businesswoman from Hong Kong. She never had much to do with the rest of us, and we speculated about why she came all the way to our little island to sit and drink all by herself. A few weeks later she would be beaten and left for dead on a jungle path behind the bar.

I was younger than most of my Hong Kong friends—not quite thirty—but I was like them in many ways. Ravaged by past experiences. Alone in the world. Confused about where I belonged. Earlier, in Berlin, I had once gone to a psychoanalyst who told me, "You're like all the other Americans who come to me. You're cut off at the roots." Looking at these damaged and dying expatriates in the bar, I saw myself: a dead plant, still green, wilting on a dark jungle path, severed at the roots. I felt—what was it?— hate, terror, despair? Whatever it was, I knew I didn't want to be one of them. Once more, I was overcome by the familiar feeling that I wanted to be gone from there. So I left. Only this time, at age twenty-eight, I went home.

Is it hope or is it despair that motivates us to leave whole lives behind us? It has to be part hope, I think. Of course, Elián Gonzales did not choose his flight, but when I envision him out there by himself in the ocean, clutching some seemingly arbitrary flotsam in an eternity of water and horror and noise, I see hope: Elián clinging, first to his mom, then to that miraculous inner tube, then to his relatives in Miami, to his protector in the closet we saw in news photos, and finally to his triumphant father on the front page of every Cuban newspaper—in short, to whatever tenuous hope might offer itself. Like him, at that moment in the bar, recognizing the misery and danger of this world, my own familiar world, and having exhausted every imaginable alternative to it, by some miracle I still clung to the hope that salvation, however vague my understanding of it might be, would yet offer itself. And I went home.

Seven years after I left Hong Kong, when I was thirty-five and still struggling against the atheism with which I had been afflicted for most of my adult life, I came upon these words in the book of Hebrews that seemed to describe my experience: "Now faith is being sure of what we hope for and certain of what we do not see" (11:1). Reading the words, I realized I *was* sure of what I hoped for—an alternative to the rottenness of this life—and I was suddenly as certain that it must exist as if I were actually seeing heaven with my own eyes.

According to the notes in the Bible, all that can be said with any assurance about the author of Hebrews is that he was writing to Jewish converts to Christianity—probably *before* the destruction of Jerusalem and the temple in 70 A.D, the notes argue, because the author omits all mention of so awful and important an event. To me, though, the definition of faith that the author of Hebrews offers belies a knowledge, or perhaps a foreknowledge, of that destruction—of the loss and terror and hate and ugliness and flight it must have resulted in—and of the realness of a hope, like Elián's, that clings fast, defying all reason, a hope that enables a mother, against every impulse and instinct of her being, to send her daughters out into some uncertain safety.

Relevant and cited scriptural passages: Exodus 1, 5, 12, and 16 and Hebrews
11:1.

Other references:

Daniel Defoe. *Robinson Crusoe.* 1719.

Anne Frank. *The Diary of a Young Girl.* 1947.

4

Hope

I became a Christian in my thirties. I wish I could say that I welcomed Jesus as my Savior from the moment I heard his name as a child and that I submitted to him eagerly and dedicated my life to glorifying him, but in truth I would have to admit that I have always struggled to remain my own boss. I had to fight him off for an entire lifetime before I finally recognized my own ridiculous inadequacy to save myself and gave up the struggle. What a joy it is to exchange fighting for rest!

The struggle began in my Catholic childhood. My family lived in California during my first seven years, then moved to a small town in Connecticut, returning when I was in high school. In those days, I knew about Jesus and his teachings from our illustrated children's Bible and my childhood catechism classes as well as from the parts of the gospel that were read during the mass. Had I been asked at any time in my growing up years, I would certainly have said and even believed that Jesus was God's son and that God loved me. I prayed when I was sad or wanted something.

I was active in the various parishes my family attended until I was in college, even serving as the sole youth member of the parish council when I was twelve. I sang in the choir when I was a child and played the banjo and sang in the church folk group throughout my high school years.

I attended a Catholic high school for two years, and my experience there was in no way like the horror stories some tell of evil nuns who ruled by fear and taught only guilt. Quite the contrary. The nuns were loving, caring, honest people genuinely dedicated to serving God by teaching us. If anything, they left out all mention of our guilt and shame in their enthusiasm for talking about loving God and following the Golden Rule.

I always loved the mass. One part of the liturgy was especially moving and important to me: the part before the communion when the priest raised the bread up and said, "This is the Lamb of God," and the congregation responded: "Lord, I am not worthy to receive you, but only say the word, and my soul shall be healed." I don't think I fully understood what the words meant then or knew the biblical event that they were derived from, but they spoke to some secret, torn part of me that even then knew I was not worthy and needed healing, and the words held a promise that the healing was possible. Still, on the surface I thought I was invulnerable, then. After all, I reasoned, I went to church and tried to do the right thing and was genuinely sorry when I didn't.

Then, during my first year of college, as I have written earlier, my mom got sick and began a slow process of dying. Coincidentally, as it seemed to me then, I stopped believing that there was a God, much less that he had a son, or that any of the other details of what had constituted my faith to that point were true. One by one, the rest of my family fell away from the church. As for me, I was not angry at God or bitter, or, if I was, I didn't know it. I just stopped believing, as immediately and as suddenly as a dropped curtain, and the only feelings I associate with this phase of my spiritual life were grief that I no longer had anyone to pray to and a strange mixture of jealous fascination and embarrassment whenever I heard Christians speak about their faith.

When my older sister Sharon took our invalid mother in to live with her, as I mentioned earlier in this book, it was no small act of mercy. The two had fought continually throughout Sharon's teenage years, seriously enough that Sharon had run away from home a few times. When I returned from abroad once a year or so to see my now scattered family for brief periods at a time, I usually stayed with Sharon, and I also started corresponding with her. I grew closer to her than I had with any other family member. Sharon had become a Christian, I learned. Then she married, and it turned out her husband was a Christian, too, and the two of them began an all out campaign to "win me to Christ."

I resisted as forcefully as diplomacy would allow. They prayed for me and tried to persuade me. I listened politely and asked a few questions and tried above all not to offend them by outright disagreeing with anything they said. I didn't want to hurt my sister's feelings, but I knew that—though I might secretly want to—I couldn't *make* myself believe something I was sure was not true. Besides, I argued with myself as well as with my sister and brother-in-law, if faith and grace were gifts of God, there was no way I could set out to gain them; he had to *give* them to me, offer them to me unbidden, and I could have no part in that.

And then there was my mom. Blind by then. Hardly able to walk or even sit up straight. Bald, but for the grizzled wisps around the edges of her face that she insisted on letting grow long. Always hungry and increasingly fat, because the operation to remove the tumor had damaged the part of her brain that regulates appetite. Incapable of remembering what she said from one moment to the next.

She, too, had become a Christian, or so Sharon told me. When I went home to see her, I would find her at my sister's kitchen table with a Bible in her lap. She couldn't read it, couldn't recognize me from my voice except, hesitantly, as "my Patty," a teenage version of myself I no longer remembered. She couldn't even hold onto any one thought except to say over and over, as confiding and joyful as a child, "Jesus loves me, Jesus loves me, Jesus loves me." It was the most pathetic sight I had ever seen, this wreck of my mom, sitting cock-eyed and broken and patting her Bible, claiming this obvious lie to be true. I was always glad to get back on the plane and leave that part of my life behind me.

Part of me hoped, though. My sister's love toward my mother spoke to me more loudly than the passages from the Bible that she and her husband made me listen to. Even after my mother was no longer aware of anything, Sharon cleaned and turned and patted and spoke to her. Sometimes she stood for a long time just holding her hand. Watching my sister from the doorway to the guestroom where our mother lay dying, part of me hoped, perhaps began to know even then, that Jesus *did* love my mom, even as she said he did.

Having lived abroad for most of my adult years, I was beginning to be disenchanted with my life as an expatriate. I had lived in Berlin, Beijing, and Hong Kong, and I began to see that the three places were alike in many regards. Most of the people I knew—both fellow expatriates and native intellectuals—seemed unhappy and directionless. Things I longed for, such as a committed love relationship and children and absolute answers to my many questions, were scorned as limitations on freedom. Nobody seemed to want to grow up. Everyone seemed to be motivated by fear and hopelessness more than by anything else. I told myself and my friends I would return to the United States to study creative writing, but my real desire was to find direction and love and hope, to feed them, to grow them.

It is amazing to me now how quickly I found them—or they found me. Within four years I was married and had two small children and lived on a farm. And one Sunday morning in the summer, when my husband and I were raking and baling our neighbor's field for hire, the neighbor showed up to see how the hay was coming and invited us to his Sunday school class at the Baptist church in the small town where we live.

I had no idea what that meant. My husband was a devout Christian—and a literalist with respect to the Bible, I was learning—but not a churchgoer. My only experience with anything one might call Sunday school was the catechism class I had had to take in order to participate in Holy Communion as a child, and adults didn't ever attend them, as far as I knew. I hadn't any idea what the Baptist faith was like. Still, we liked our neighbor, so we told him we might go to his class sometime and returned to our haying, and some weeks later we did. The class, referred to as the "old marrieds," was in actuality a collection of outcasts from the other Sunday school classes who didn't want to follow the regular Baptist Sunday school lessons with all the answers in them, using instead Disciplers study guides that made you look up the answers yourself. The couples were older than we were, but not ancient, and very lively in their discussions. They were studying the book of Hebrews.

Hebrews was slow going for the beginning student I found myself to be, full of knotty passages about things that I had never known were at issue for Christians. The book, I was told, was written to Jews in the early church, and one of the men in the class kept pointing out that it was therefore not applicable to us. But the more I read of Hebrews, the more I found it to be applicable to *me* anyway, because Hebrews defines faith as confidently hoping for God's promises to be fulfilled. That, in any case, is how I understood the first verse of Hebrews 11: "Now faith is being sure of what we hope for and certain of what we do not see."

I was becoming pretty comfortable with hoping, by that time. I had hoped myself home from a miserable future abroad. I had hoped myself into a marriage and through two pregnancies and into a gratifying career teaching writing. I had hoped myself into a growing community of loving Christians who entertained my questions and wouldn't give up praying for my surrender. Secretly, I hoped my sister was right in what she believed and that my mom was in heaven with the Jesus who loved her. Most of all, I realized I had been hoping for a long time that God would speak but the word that my soul might be healed. And then I realized that he *had* spoken it, that the very book I studied—the book that my mother had patted under the kitchen table—*was* his word, composed over centuries to keep our hope alive, and that his son Jesus was the *living* word, the living proof and the promise that our hoping was not in vain.

It would still be a while before I realized how badly I botch things when I try to run my life and even longer before I gave up trying. In fact, I still struggle against myself. Also, this is but one current in a confluence of events through which God pulled me to him in my lifetime. He pulls me yet, ever toward him, away from where I would go without his hand to drag me back, and it gives me a wonderful feeling of certainty to be held fast.

Relevant and cited scriptural passages: Isaiah 64:6, Matthew 6:6 and 8:5–13, and Hebrews 11:1.

5

Entering the Fortress

I've been trying for years to find a good biography of Martin Luther, but they're all boring and badly written. Typically, they're more about the Catholic church and dense theological debates than they are about the man himself. And, while the church was fascinatingly corrupt in those days and its theologians as diverting as they are to this day, I miss the man in it all: the hand that held the hammer; the voice that first sang the words of one of Christendom's most famous hymns, "A Mighty Fortress Is Our God"; the intellect that fought, quite literally, with Satan and referred to him as a worm. I want to know the stout, rather crazed looking man of Lucas Cranach's portraits—sitting slightly askew, his expression quizzical, as if he's just heard something new and different and he's getting ready to consider it.

For those of you who don't know, the story of Martin Luther goes like this. He was born of thriving peasants—that is, rural trades-people—hardworking and frugal and familiar to us in their desire to have a son who did better than they did, as they thought: they saved up their pfennigs and sent him to law school. You've met them.

Martin was a good student and was about to graduate when, one day, on his walk home from a long week at the university, he got caught in a thunderstorm and was in fear for his life. For my own part, having been raised in the mild climate of Southern California, where lightening is an anomaly and nobody walks anywhere, I would find Martin's fear extreme if I hadn't married an Oklahoman farmer. We used to farm full time. Whenever we were making hay and it started raining, his mom would come driving out in the field in the pickup to fetch us, and the whole drive back she would tell us her seventy-five years' worth of stories of people struck and maimed by lightening. I'm sure Martin's parents had told him the same stories. In any case, in his fear he made a vow to enter the monastery if he survived. Many of us have made similar vows in distressing circumstances, but Martin went on to keep his, much to his parents' disappointment. Not that they were not good Christians. It's just that they had set their hearts on this son carrying on their name and supporting them in their old age. They were angry. Martin was determined. You know how that goes.

At the monastery, though, Martin was a wreck. He worried all the time about his sinfulness. Who wouldn't worry, having trashed the education one's parents could ill afford in order to pursue a career they were against? He practiced certain monastic remedies for sinful behavior: he fasted and tortured himself and attended church services several times a day. He had a mentor who genuinely cared about him and to whom he confessed his sins daily. His mentor was so impressed with Martin's apparent piety that he made him a monastic priest, able to conduct the services that everyone else merely attended. But none of this made Martin feel any better. In fact, it made him feel even worse: he was a hypocrite, merely going through the motions of a faith he found increasingly unpersuasive. He even told his mentor that he had no faith and blasphemed repeatedly to prove it. His mentor responded by sending him back to the university to study and eventually teach scripture. There was a need at a nearby university for a professor to teach the Bible, and Martin, he was sure, was their man.

What is it about mentor types that they seem to see through our struggles? Is it the process of mentoring? The relationship? Or is it the Holy Spirit's way of speaking to us when we're so busy groaning and wailing we can't even hear what we ourselves are saying? In any case, there couldn't have been a better solution to Martin's spiritual dilemma. He was fighting with God; he needed to study God.

Now I need to stop here and tell you that I don't buy the whole argument that Martin was fighting with the Holy Roman Catholic church, not God. That's so minor compared to what was really at issue. It wasn't with the trappings of faith that Martin had his problem. The question he asked was more personal and basic: How can I—a struggler, a bad Christian, a sinner, a blasphemer, for Pete's sake—deserve salvation? Everything he had learned up to that point said he didn't, and still something in him yet hoped that this wasn't true.

And so, Martin bowed to the authority of his mentor and took up the Bible with the intention of teaching courses on Psalms and Paul's writings in a year's time. In Paul's letter to the Romans, to Martin's astonishment, he found the answer he had been looking for all along: that we *don't* deserve salvation, that there's nothing we can do to earn it, that it's merely because God's so good-natured that we can aspire to heaven at all. All we need to do to be saved is to believe that God loved us anyway, so much so that he came up with a way to him that didn't require anything at all from us. It was the answer on which the Church as Martin knew it had been founded, but one that had been forgotten, one that has been repeatedly forgotten since then by believers and churches. Although we follow in Martin's footsteps, we nevertheless lag into thinking that we have to do something in order to be worthy of eternity. We think we have to be good. Or perform some sacrament. Or be baptized. Or not engage in whatever sin is currently most looked down upon. Or evangelize our neighbors—or, better yet, people on the other side of the world. We forget what Jesus told his disciples and us: "The work of God is this: to believe in the one he has sent."

This discovery broke everything apart for Martin, just as it does for anyone who makes the same discovery to this day: *I'm scum, but God loves me—go figure.* Like the woman at the well, Martin wanted everyone to know about it right away, and he sure wanted the Church to know it and quit coming up with requirements for salvation that sought to contradict it. And so came the nailing of the ninety-five theses on the church door and all those academic debates about whether one could bribe one's way into heaven and if a human being such as the pope could stand between a believer and God. Martin spent some time hiding from authorities, because, of course, they didn't much like being told they shouldn't solicit money from believers. Even Protestants don't like being told this, I might add, judging from the number of sermons I've heard in my few years as a Christian defending the collection of tithes. But for the most part, Martin wouldn't shut up.

Somewhere in the midst of the theological turmoil and public debate, Martin Luther holed up in a castle and painstakingly translated the entire Bible into plain, easy-to-read German. You need to understand that this is the translation, with minor modernizations, still read by German-speaking believers today. The language is so simple that I, a non-native speaker of German with less than two years of formal training, can read and understand it with ease. Not only was the translation of Scripture into the language of the uneducated a major part of Luther's goal of making the availability of salvation known to all, but the project fertilized his own growth as a Christian. Luther grew solider in his faith as well as in his physical stature. He became more likeable and real.

Luther lived under a constant death threat for his ideas in a time when many less radical religious thinkers and translators of scripture were summarily martyred. Nevertheless, his biography reads like a comic novel, if you can get past all the debates and indulgences, decrials and papal bulls—which, like the Diet of Worms, are a lot less fun to read about than they sound. He was defrocked, then formally excommunicated, but went around in the flowing robes of his monk's habit anyway. He spoke like a jolly rube and journaled compulsively. How refreshing to hear a theologian engage the vulgar, as so many of the original biblical writers did! He called his enemies from Rome "papal asses" and reveled in farting at the devil and described, in that passionate detail born of suffering and catharsis, his myriad gastrointestinal difficulties. He earned his living by writing and had a bevy of students and ex-monks as followers, and they swarmed around him in his low-ceilinged living room, arguing and joking and studying scripture.

Soon a group of nuns wanted to join them, but there was a problem: if they left the convent, they'd have to have somewhere to live and someone to provide for them. Luther snuck into their convent yard by night with a wagon full of barrels in which he hid them and carried them away to his house, where all thirteen of them lived until he found husbands for them among his followers. For all but one, that is, Katharina of Bora, who, at twenty-six, no one seemed to want. After two attempts to match her up failed, Katharina joked that Luther himself ought to take her. He had all sorts of excuses. At forty-two he was too old, he was sure to be martyred soon, he didn't have enough money, etc., but in the end his parents insisted that he needed a wife to carry on their name, so he married her.

Katharina contributed significantly to the household. In addition to producing six children, two of whom died, she brewed beer, raised livestock, and rented out a piece of land she owned. She also fed and looked after the students who still hung out at their house and drank beer and debated and grew in their faith. Some of them lived with the Luthers, as did various of Katharina's relatives and her sister's six children. At sixty-three, Martin Luther died, a happy man. Now that was a well-lived life.

Say that you admire Martin Luther these days, and you'll be told he was an anti-Semite, which is true. In his younger years he defended the Jews and wanted them to profit from the promise of salvation that he, like they, had had such trouble understanding at first. But in his later years, as many do, Luther became a flat-out racist. He despised the Jews and published diatribes against them recommending heinous actions embarrassingly similar to those later perpetrated by the Nazis. Indeed, the Nazis used Luther's views, quoted shockingly verbatim in their pronouncements, to justify their own. There is no way to rationalize Luther's racist attitudes or make them right. They're not. He was wrong. Shamefully evil. Good thing God didn't require that he be perfect.

The key thing to know about Martin Luther, I think, is that every event of his life—like every event in yours and mine—was part of the vining growth plan of ups and downs God had devised for him. God frightened him, pushed him, wound him round the Word. As with Noah and Hezekiah and Jonah and others, many of the downturns of Luther's life happened toward the end, when you'd think he'd be past all that badness, past his humanness, a completely godly man, producing the fullest and most mellow fruit. But it's God's plan, not ours, after all, and we are not his equal. As Job points out, "Who can bring what is pure from the impure? No one!"—no one except God, of course, who can do the impossible and did it with me and goes around doing it all the time.

Relevant and cited scriptural passages: Job 14:4; Psalm 46; Mark 10:27; John 3:16, 6:29, and 10:10; and Romans, especially 3–6 and 8:22–27.

Other references:

Martin Luther. "A Mighty Fortress Is Our God." 1529.

Lucas Cranach the Elder. Luther portrait. Circa 1529.

6

On Being Cleaned

Consciousness of sin, as I have said, played little role in my initial conversion to faith. Still, as I read through the Bible in the years following my conversion—beginning, of course, at the beginning as I would any other book—it at one point occurred to me that I had thus far in my life violated not only most of the lesser sins of obstinacy, greed, and selfishness that Moses goes on about but just about every one of the Ten Commandments. This was an unsettling thought. Even though as a growing believer I was becoming increasingly confident that I would not be held accountable, neither for my past sins nor for any I would yet commit, I nevertheless began to feel embarrassingly dirty—the kind of dirty you feel when you are in a public place and suddenly realize you smell bad—and my dirtiness became a secret and increasingly consuming source of pain to me.

One day during those years, popular evangelist Tony Campolo spoke during chapel at my university about how, during his private time with Jesus in the morning, he didn't pray anything and God didn't tell him anything. Rather, he just allowed Jesus to cleanse him through his presence. He compared the feeling with Blaise Pascal's ecstatic response to his own conversion: "Fire! Fire! Joy! Fire!" And he described Jesus repeatedly as a supernatural sponge that, when he touched Tony, instantly absorbed all the sin and ugliness out Tony's body into his own. It was, like most of Tony's images during this fabulous sermon, a powerful but unusual metaphor for the ministering of grace, not the pouring out that we usually imagine but a magical sucking-in process.

I couldn't help seeing in my mind as he spoke the only adult occasion on which I was washed by another person. It was when I was in the hospital about to have my first child. I lay between contractions in my own mess of amniotic fluid and unintended urine in a strange high bed, surrounded by nurses dabbing at me while my visitors watched.

It is a thing we don't speak of openly, the messiness of birth that is our curse. New moms sometimes go on about the intensity of their pain or even embarrass their more modest listeners with detailed accounts of their extended labor. "My water broke," they might tell us. Or, "They had to induce labor because my contractions were too weak." Or, "I was only dilated three centimeters after twenty-four hours of labor!" Mostly, though, we just don't talk about these matters. Some say, although this is a lie, that the mother forgets the pain of childbirth; otherwise she wouldn't be able to go through the process another time. We do, however, stop telling the pain and concentrate instead on the amazing fact of the birth itself, the new life that emerges like a phoenix from these horrifying details.

When my sisters and brothers and I were children, my mom told us more than once that the birth of a child was the most beautiful event she had ever witnessed. I don't know how it came to be that she was present at a birth; we never asked about that. What we wanted were the gory details—that it came out head first, the goo it was covered with, that it really came out from down there! But my mother—a woman who rued her own many children for demoting her from career engineer to housewife—even in giving us the dirt on the birth she had witnessed, had this holy look on her face, a reverence I only ever saw when she spoke of creation.

Once she dragged me out to the atrium to see some newborn weeds that had mysteriously sprouted overnight in a brand-new planter of store-bought potsoil. Another time she went into ecstasies of delight over the perfectly spherical little poops our rabbit had left in a trail down our carpet when he got in the house. She held them out in her hand to show me and a visiting friend, as if they were precious stones. "Aren't they amazing? So round! Aren't they just perfect?"

I was in my mid teens then, about the time when I was beginning to be embarrassed about everything she did, about the time when we would discover the gigantic tumor in the middle of her brain. After the operation, she had to stay in the hospital for a long time.

I thought about this hospital stay, too, as Tony Campolo talked. My mother was a different creature in the hospital than she had ever been. She was swollen, for one—her face so enlarged by all the cutting and sawing and drugs that she had none of her old features or wrinkles but looked as smooth and round-faced as a baby. I can't tell you how disconcerting this was. Even before she woke from her weeks-long sleep following the surgery to become the increasingly handicapped child-woman she was until her death eleven years later, she looked like a new person to me. Rescued from death. A new birth. Redeemed.

Redeemed wasn't something we talked about in my growing up years, so I probably didn't actually think that then. For Catholics, words like *redemption* and *sin* only ever came up in church, and then minus the gory details of what they really meant. And anyway, redeemed would have been too positive a description of my mom's new self. In that hospital room, my mother was waking up to a new life of being dressed and undressed and fed and washed by other people.

The nurses, I remember, offered to massage her.

"It's good for people," they said, "the hands on."

But my mom wasn't having any of it, and she didn't like them washing her either. She set her jaw, for a second looking like her old self again, and told us, "I don't want some stranger touching me."

When Tony Campolo spoke of that sponge, I thought of my mom, helpless on that bed, not wanting to be touched. How wonderful it would be, I was thinking, if it could be as Tony said—if we could be cleansed by a magic sponge that hardly needed to touch us to soak up the sin from our rank bodies. But I fear it is not so. Being cleansed takes touching, hands-on, firm, probing pressure. To be cleansed, one must submit to being exposed to the one doing the cleansing. Being cleansed means allowing someone—some cleaner, more adept, more powerful other person—to manhandle one's dignity.

Peter knew this when he balked at Jesus washing his feet. I know we always read Peter's initial refusal as horror at Jesus so humbling himself to do the work of a servant, but consider why it was a slave's job to wash feet to begin with. If you have to have others examine the mixture of dirt and manure and spit on your feet or touch the fungus growing between your toes, you want them to be beneath you, people accustomed to dirty things, people you can regard as dirt themselves. How humiliating it would be to have one's hero or even some elegantly clad and shod person stoop to grab one's naked foot and scrub it clean. I have never been able to understand how a person could stand to have a pedicure for this reason. How could I let my beautician, with her coiffed hair and dainty fingers and sweet fragrance, mess around with my feet?

To me, the prospect of being cleansed and even healed requires surrendering one's dignity. It requires submitting oneself to some-one else's appraising gaze. It amounts to shame.

It's good to keep things in perspective—to remember the birth, the health, the cleanness that results—and not dwell on the ugly realities of the process. But just imagine how that woman felt who touched the hem of Jesus' cloak. Mark tells us, "Immediately her bleeding stopped and she felt in her body that she was freed from her suffering" (5:29). Just as if immediately Tony Campolo's supernatural sponge had absorbed not only the blood but her suf-fering as well.

But still the woman didn't get away clean. Jesus first questioned the crowd, who all—including the woman—denied anything happened. Only upon "seeing that she could not go unnoticed" did the woman fall "trembling" (Luke 8:47) at Jesus' feet. And only after she explained what happened "In the presence of all the people"—that is to say, only after she revealed her menstrual problems to a crowd of her neighbors—did Jesus allow her to go in peace. In front of everyone, he exposed her private misery, the disgraceful humanness that made her a pariah in Jewish society and that repulses us to this day. Blood. Illness. Filth. Pain. Before she could enjoy the holy wonder of health and cleanness and new life, she had to undergo shame.

And so I listened to Tony with awe and envy and longing. I

believe he was telling the truth. Perhaps his ecstatic experience of miraculous cleansing unsullied by shame comes from the fact that, as he told us, he can't remember a time when he didn't know Jesus. I can. And I can remember the many times when, having finally come to know him, I forgot all about him. My sins are as nasty and inescapable as bodily fluids and dirt. To get really clean, I need a thorough going over, and that's never an easy thing.

Relevant and cited scriptural passages: Matthew 9:20–22, Mark 5:25–34, Luke 8:43–48, and John 13:1–17.

Other references:

Blaise Pascal. Journal entries describing his 23 November 1654 conversion.

Tony Campolo. Staley Spiritual Awareness lectures. John Brown University. 12–14 September 2000.

Struggling

7

The Eyes of Faith

We often talk about Jesus as the "Great Physician," although I know of no evidence that he was actually in the medical profession. He did do healings, but, then, we don't call those healers we see on TV "physicians," do we? Sometimes, though, I like to imagine Jesus as an actual doctor. My doctor. My ophthalmologist, maybe. Let's say I have some trouble with my eyes—like the corneal ulcer I had a few years ago, a little inexplicable hole in the slick surface of the eye—and Dr. Christ drops the burning yellow dye in my eye to get a better look at it and then tells me, "You have eyes, but cannot see," or something even more alarming. Now there's a scary place to go!

The Christian life is all about correct vision. We want to be people whose eyes see clearly, unlike those faithless outsiders Jesus talks about in Mark 4, who are always seeing but never perceiving, seeing God's invisible qualities everywhere they look but never being certain of what it all means, staring straight at Jesus but somehow not noticing the messy wounds in his hands, the dark stain at his side. Or not caring. We don't want to be like that. And so we study. We lean in to see more clearly what is at best only duskily before us. We squint. We rub our eyes, close them for a moment, and look again.

The Bible offers us many kinds of eyes—eyes that see clearly, eyes overflowing with tears, eyes with scales on them, eyes with planks in them, eyes darker than wine, eyes that should be gouged out, eyes that are lamps, eyes that hate the hands or the feet or secretly envy other body parts, eyes that cause us to sin, eyes too small for a camel or a rich man to pass through, and lustful eyes, painted eyes, eyes that offend us, eyes with barbs in them, eyes that see treasure, eyes that see destruction, eyes that are on all of creation from the beginning of the year to the end. People make covenants with their eyes. They open their eyes, close their eyes, wipe their eyes, and lift up their eyes to the mountains. The blind are made to see, and the sighted become blind because of sin or drought or sheer stupidity. Both good things and bad things are pleasing to the eye, and seeing is metaphorical for everything from sinning to repenting to understanding. Ironically, there are blind watchmen, as well as blind men, who are the only ones who can see. Through our eyes we are enlightened and also led astray.

What are we to make of it all? How, as Christians, do we take on this burden—described by Jesus as "light"—of seeing the way God would have us see? Is seeing through the eyes of faith the same thing as what many Christians tell me they are trying to do—that is, seeing ourselves as God sees us? And how is that, exactly? Does he see me as I see my own children, as flawed, horrible even, but utterly lovable because they are mine? Or does he see only our sins, those bloody rags we drag after us? Does the All-Seeing One see only the part that doesn't offend him, the purity of Jesus in us? I have been offered each of these possibilities. Just how do we go about being students of God? What do we look at? And what should we do about what we see? Is closing our eyes a correct or faithful way of seeing?

We are a culture of seers. We take our vision so seriously that we put glasses on babies and routinely correct even the slightest imperfection in our own eyes. We insert slivers of glass or plastic into our eyes or, worse, allow doctors to slice our eyeballs open to make us see better. After all, sight is essential to almost everything we do—driving, reading, welding, sewing, learning, making art, working on a computer. Faced with imminent blindness, we imagine our daily lives slamming to a mystifying halt. We couldn't live and move and have our being the way we normally do. We couldn't see *or* perceive. We couldn't recognize the visible, much less the invisible, in the world around us. And so we protect our vision and see it as an essential.

What does faith see? For that, we must return, I think, to the moment when we saw by faith for the very first time. In that moment, we saw differently than we ever had seen before. We had x-ray vision then. We were able to see through the things of this world and recognize in them God's invisible qualities—love, order, patience, enthusiasm—revealed in the world he created for our benefit. Faith, after all, merely confirms what creation shows us in that first lightning bolt of believing. We looked at apples, grass, shade and saw provision. We looked at algebra and saw order. We looked at our pain and struggles, even our terror, and recognized God's patience and his amazing gift of free will.

To see by faith, we must return to that day, that week, that month perhaps, when our ordinary sight was still stunned by that new way of seeing, when everything was still blurrily, blindingly bright. Like the woman at the well, in our first recognition of truth, we saw everything we previously knew in a different way, and we acted on it. We left our water jars behind in our excitement to tell others whom we had previously envied but now looked upon as desperately thirsty for the same living water that quenched us. In that first bright bright moment, we saw our hopes as certainties and those old promises as truth. For a short time, blinded to our old way of seeing, everything we did and said and saw and felt seemed to be about God. And only later, when the truth dimmed and settled to the vague glow of memory beneath our current preoccupations, did we lose that way of seeing. Only later did it seem that church was church, God was God, and everything else was, well, everything else, where seeing didn't matter—except when myopia or cataracts or macular degeneration or corneal ulcers got in the way of it.

Relevant and cited scriptural passages: Psalm 17:7, Jeremiah 14:6, Mark
    4:10–20, John 4:1–42, Acts 17:28, Romans 1:20, and 1 Corinthians 13:12.

8

Down by the Riverside

Every once in a while, not very often and not nearly as often as I probably should for good bonding, I take one of my daughters out on a date. It's usually a Saturday morning, and my husband Kris takes the other one, and we generally meet up somewhere afterwards before returning home to our normal afternoon routine of playtime, dinner, bath, playtime, story, then bed. The idea of it, just mother and daughter going off somewhere together, as grownups do, is often more exciting for both of us than the reality of it.

We choose a venture more mature than the typical child activity, such as eating at a fancier than usual restaurant, and throughout our special time together we linger to do things my children refer to as "romantic," like sharing a huge bowl of wonton soup, even though neither of them likes such complicated food mixtures, or eating fast food in the car, which is otherwise strictly prohibited in our family. These romances are premeditated and usually entertain some ordinarily loathsome or forbidden element, some demonstration that we are free from quotidian habits and rules. We talk differently to each other: carefully, asking more questions, offering each other more choices than is our wont. Although not by design, we talk to each other as people might on a real date, our exchanges tentative and somewhat stilted, as if we have only just met or don't know each other at all. Our awkwardness contributes, I think, to the emotional delicacy of these dates. All is precarious; everything can go kipping over with the most minor misstep.

On one such date, when Charlotte was six, I took her dress shopping as a prize for ten consecutive days and nights of not sucking her thumb. She wanted a grown-up dress, by which I understood she meant a silky, swirly one with lace. Although she's generally not a lacy dress kind of child and would probably wear it only once or twice, I thought buying such a dress would be positive reinforcement. Grown-ups don't suck their thumbs, I reasoned.

Actually, some do. My mother-in-law has told me this and has been telling me this ever since Charlotte was a baby and, disdaining pacifiers, I let her suck her little thumb in the first place. It seems that Mamaw, as we call her, had a college roommate some fifty years ago who sucked her thumb and twirled a lock of hair whenever she studied in the semi-secrecy of their shared room. Nina Harding was the girl's name. She had a little wisp of blond hair that grew from her crown that she had twirled short. She wore it straight off, according to Mamaw.

So, on this date, Charlotte and I drive to the mall at Fayetteville, forty-five minutes away, the closest big town to where we live. Before we make it out of the driveway, we plan our morning. We will not listen to Dr. Laura on the radio but instead a tape of kids' songs. Charlotte will get a grown-up dress, but Lulu won't get one because she hasn't done anything special to deserve it, and she's still a baby anyway. My daughter makes me promise that her little sister won't get a lacy grown-up dress.

She is hungry, she tells me. This can't be, because it's only 10:00 a.m., and she just ate waffles and bacon for breakfast. She suggests we eat fish sandwiches for lunch—my favorite, which Charlotte generally hates—and french fries with ketchup from the drive-through. Should we stop at a gas station and buy beef jerky on the way home? Or should we share a banana split at Braums? I tell her we have only four hours before we have to meet Daddy and Lulu at Barnes and Noble, so we may not be able to do everything this time.

After this discussion, for a long time, we are silent, watching the dry yellow roadside curve by us. If it were summer, it would be shaggy with wildflowers. Charlotte chews Dentyne to keep from getting carsick. She hangs a piece out from between her teeth as she chews, the way my dad always did when I was a kid and he was trying for the hundredth time to quit smoking.

Raffi sings as we drive. *Gonna lay down my sword and shield, down by the riverside.* It reminds Charlotte of the David and Goliath episode of *Wishbone*, a PBS program she and Lulu watch at Mamaw's house every day after school. Having never really watched it myself, I have never managed to get the straight of how the show works except that human actors and a real dog act out classic works of literature. The dog is always the protagonist, and I've had glimpses of him at his work, proposing to Elizabeth Bennett or turning away in horror as Sidney Carton's head—actually a cabbage—rolls from the guillotine. TV has gotten more difficult to explain since I was a kid. Ever since my daughters started watching *Wishbone*, they have amazed me by their knowledge of and interest in the major plot lines and even minor characters' names from many of the same novels I teach to college students. Charlotte is amused when Goliath tells David, "You think you're a boy come with your little stick to fight me?" She tries to explain what she found so funny about this, and it has to do with the fact that the dog is throwing a stick at a boy, when usually boys throw sticks to dogs.

"That's a pun, isn't it, Mama?" she asks me. Not wanting to show her up or have to explain situational irony to a six-year-old and also impressed that she got a joke I probably would have missed, I concede. She also remembers the dog's response, verbatim: "You come with a sword and a shield, and I come in the army of the Lord." *Down by the riverside*, I hum to myself.

We enter the mall through Sears and begin to make the rounds. Everything Charlotte likes is made out of polyester, which I hate. It's like wearing plastic, I tell her. She is hungry, she reminds me, and wants to go get the fish sandwiches right away. I don't want to leave so soon, now that we're at the mall, so I suggest we get them at the food court as soon as we've shopped this wing. The features of my daughter's face go flat as a picture, but she says okay.

We continue to shop, but with a desultory inattention to the original plan. No more twirling of clothes racks or wistful fingering of cloth. We look at snow globes now and sniff at scented candles rimmed with dust, leftovers from Christmas piled up on card tables covered with red felt tablecloths. The trip has soured suddenly, irreparably it seems. It is as though we have each found out some unpleasant defect in the other, a crucial flaw demanding censure that we didn't know about beforehand.

At the mouth of a blacklit store featuring lava lamps and hermit crabs climbing their cages, Charlotte slips on the slick tiles and almost falls. Several shoppers reach out toward her out of instinct, as I do, but she jerks herself away from the hands. Especially my hands. She is furious at me. My daughters are always furious at me when they get hurt or embarrassed, and this has always puzzled and offended me.

"Why are you blaming me?" I ask her. "I didn't do anything."

She just glares at me and stomps on ahead toward the food court. I am dreading this meal. If I were dead with hunger, I wouldn't want a fish sandwich right now.

Then, suddenly, the answer to years of hurt wondering comes to me, like an unexpected kiss, and I feel good again and full of hope.

"I know why you're mad," I tell her back. She ignores me. I skip to catch up with her.

"Is it because I didn't keep you from slipping?" I ask, knowing.

She turns and opens her eyes wide and purses her mouth at my statement of the obvious. But I now know the truth, and the knowledge of it sings inside of me: my daughters hold me responsible, me alone, for their happiness. They expect miracles and protection from me, as from some hero from an old romance. In their eyes, I can do marvelous feats and prevent disaster. I am right and just, always right and just. And for now this is a wonderful thing. Charlotte will grow out of this absolute faith in me. I will want her to. But for now, for an instant, I know how God must feel when we turn to him, even in anger as Job did, and expect only good things at his hand. There is nothing like a child's trust.

Later, after a lunch of chicken nuggets and a shared strawberry frulatti, we buy two little stuffed dogs on key chains, one for her and one for Lulu. They are in a bin of sale items outside Gymboree, where we made our last unsuccessful attempt to find the perfect grownup dress, and they cost $1.49 apiece. Charlotte takes her time selecting the dogs. They have to be similar, but not identical: one sitting, one standing, different colors. She chooses the bigger one for herself, even though it's purple, Lulu's color. The dog she chooses for Lulu is yellow and orange with a patch over one eye, just like Wishbone.

From this point on, all Charlotte wants to do is go to Barnes and Noble and give Lulu her dog. My husband and I enter the store with our children simultaneously from different entrances, and the two girls run at each other from opposite ends of the store, almost embracing, as if they haven't seen each other in forever. Lulu holds out a glittering plastic monstrosity, a star castle with a glittery plastic key that opens it to reveal a tiny mermaid, a dolphin, and two even tinier fish. Charlotte hides the two little dogs behind her back.

"Which hand?" she asks her sister, but Lulu only wants to show off the star castle and how you unlock it and all of its little cubbyholes and interior doors that really open. The turrets come off to make bubble wands, and the deep towers are receptacles for bubble liquid. When Charlotte finally gives her sister the little dog, Lulu hardly glances at it before stuffing it in her pocket, and then the two of them are back to admiring the castle.

"Daddy got it as my prize," Lulu tells Charlotte, proudly.

"But it's really for *both* of us," Charlotte counters. I cringe at the approaching battle, the familiar ranging of the weapons, but Lulu surprises me.

"Uh huh," she says, just exactly as if she knows this is the right thing to do. Then they disappear together down the long central aisle into the kids' books, with Kris and me following.

Romance is a funny thing, created by fantasy but subject to an appreciation of propriety. Once, at Braums I overheard an acquaintance ordering peanut cluster ice cream. He was the last in a large group of people, a family with many children, for whom he was buying double cones.

"We only have that flavor in summer, sir. I'm sorry," the weary woman behind the glass told him, not sounding very sorry. A milky scoop in one hand, she held the glass cover of the freezer open with the other while she waited for him to make up his mind.

"Only in summer," the man mused, as though the idea pleased him. "How romantic."

We didn't get to do any of the things Charlotte wanted to do on our date. We didn't get a dress, didn't eat fish sandwiches in the car. After the bookstore, we did have ice cream, but we didn't share a banana split. My husband and I switched kids and drove separately to Braums. Once there, the girls got what they always get: Lulu a single dip brownie sundae and Charlotte a strawberry shortcake sundae, double dip because the cake comes that big and they won't cut it in half. As always, we tried to talk her out of it, saying she couldn't possibly eat that much. As always, she held firm.

"I can eat it all," Charlotte told us. And she did. She wouldn't give me even a single bite.

Relevant and cited scriptural passages: 1 Samuel 17 and Job.
Other references:
Raffi. "Down by the Riverside." *Bananaphone*. 1994.
"Little Big Dog." *Wishbone*. PBS. 1995.

9

The Treasures of Darkness, Part 1

Once Charlotte lamented to me that she only ever felt like "God was really there" very occasionally. Sometimes during the singing part of church, she said, (never during the *talking* part, she emphasized), and then sometimes during certain weather conditions, such as when the sun breaks through the clouds and makes light come down like fingers. At those times, she said, she feels suddenly happy, even if she had been sad or mad at somebody a moment before, and then she knows that God is there.

I commiserated with her. I don't always "feel" the presence of God, I said, as she so obviously yearned to, and I, too, wished I felt his presence every moment of the day and night. But, I told her, that doesn't mean I think he's gone whenever I don't feel him there.

"It's like me loving you," I said. "I'm not there every second of your day, and even when I am there you don't always notice me. Like if you're reading or watching a movie or out in the yard with the dogs. Or maybe we're mad at each other, and you're off in your room, and I'm stomping around the kitchen. Still, even in those moments you know that I exist and I'm there and I love you."

She agreed, but I could see from the blank longing in her face that my answer didn't satisfy her.

Actually, what I wanted to tell my daughter—but didn't—was the truth about the presence of God in my experience: that, with very few and precious exceptions, I have felt his presence most concretely and steadfastly at the absolute worst times of my life. I wanted to tell her that most of the instances when I actually *felt* the presence of God were anything but pleasant and happy experiences. Rather, they were times of struggle.

Perhaps it is a negative way of looking at things, but I see my past life—physically, emotionally, and spiritually speaking—as a series of struggles. When I was Charlotte's age, I struggled with the dilemmas and requirements of my child world. Escaping the anger and chaos of a large family. Being heard over the loud voices of my five siblings. Obeying my often unpredictable parents. Worrying about being like others and about not being like others. Worshipping people who turned out to be humans. Disobeying.

God, as I knew him in my childhood, was all about the needs and desires behind my struggles. I was aware of him watching and listening to me. I have one very distinct memory of being in a motel in Palm Springs with my family during a family vacation. My sisters and I shared a room with Venetian blinds on the one long window, and I couldn't sleep because the light of the busy street outside the window sliced in through the closed slats, breaking the darkness into moving strips of brightness as cars passed. I lay there in the eerie fragmentary dark of the strange room and suddenly knew, with the certainty of a prophet, that God saw in through the closed blinds and further still, into my very thoughts. I was aware of his presence then. He was with me—listening, caring, paying attention, eavesdropping.

Later, though, starting college in the midst of the family traumas mentioned earlier, I lost my faith. I can't really tell you what it means to lose one's faith, and I know that many believe it's not possible to do so—that, if you are able to lose your faith, then it wasn't faith to begin with. But I know that there was a time when, like Charlotte, I trusted in God and spoke to him and meant it—and then a time afterwards when I longed to trust and speak to him but couldn't. I simply no longer recognized him. Like a light that had gone out, my faith just left me. I don't remember feeling angry about it, just sad and bereft. Praying was like talking into a receiver after the other person has hung up. *Are you there? Are you there?* I kept asking, but from the silence on the other end, I knew he was gone.

Jesus became a story that solved nothing—a name from history or perhaps our fantasies, as some of my college professors seemed to believe. I felt, in a sense, like Jacob or Jonah or Job: I had asked God some hard question—What's your name? Who are you? Why don't you do what I want? How come you make me suffer?—and he refused to tell me, or else I refused to listen to his hard answers, and so I struggled.

You need to understand I was not a believer at all during this time. Perhaps I had never been. And it was a long long time. Over half my life, as I write these words. And yet, paradoxically, during those years of struggle, not believing in him, not seeing him, having no faith at all, I nevertheless felt him there. He was present in my anger. Present in my loneliness. Present in my world's refusal to be what I wanted it to be, and present in his own denial of anything I wanted to make him into. Present. With me. Patiently waiting for me to turn and see him. And still I struggled.

I don't enjoy struggling. I don't even enjoy watching it. Some people do. Some people like to watch wrestling or boxing matches, for example, and others even like to wrestle or box themselves. I flat out can't understand people like that. It pains me to see my students struggle in my classes. When we are talking about something that stretches them, and some student gets angry or has trouble even talking about whatever it is because it's such an area of struggle for him or her, I can hardly watch. I wake in the night worrying about that person's progress toward the goal of discovering truth, of knowing God.

I even get horribly embarrassed when people are struggling but don't realize it. I can't go to talent shows for this reason. At a public school where I worked for a while, I had to attend one just about every semester. Inevitably, the tape recorder fails, and some poor kid warbles blithely into the sudden silence, then stops. Worse, though, is when someone fights in vain to get in key or to recover from a fall, and the audience murmurs in embarrassment or simply has no response at all, and yet the singer or the gymnast grins on through to the end of her routine. I suffer for that person so horribly that I cry in public and have to leave.

My own struggles are the worst, though. When I contend with others or God or myself, I usually get physically sick. It's that bad. I can't sleep. My digestive system flips out in a variety of ways I'll leave to your imagination. I obsess about whatever it is I'm struggling with and can think of nothing else. One time when God and I were working on my arrogance—which, by the way, we are still working on—my forehead and cheeks and neck broke out all over in acne, a condition I have otherwise never had in my life. In moments like these, God is right there with me. I feel his presence as at no other time. I can no more ignore him than I can *not* see the world before me, the sky and the trees and the trash on the roadside.

I almost told my little daughter all of this, but then I thought that it might inhibit her desire to know God better or make her think that feeling his presence, if it's that unpleasant, must be a bad thing. It would be the kind of logical conclusion a child might come to.

My Christian college students long to feel God's presence, too. Some have spoken my daughter Charlotte's very words to me. They want and most claim to have "a personal relationship with God," a relationship that I'm guessing is something like the other personal relationships they are exploring or at least desirous of having at this point in their lives. One involving holding hands and staring into each other's eyes and being clasped in each other's arms.

The songs we sing in chapel are all about such a relationship. We sing to God, "Oh Lord, you are beautiful. Your face is all I see," and "If I could just sit with you awhile, if you could just hold me, moment by moment till forever passes by."

Such sentiments could come right out of the picture of an eternal love relationship in Marvell's famous seventeeth century carpe diem poem, "To His Coy Mistress." Without the constraints of time, the speaker in the poem tells his love, "we would sit down, and think which way / To walk and pass our long love's day." In a world unbound by aging and death, he would spend years and centuries and ages gazing upon each of his beloved's body parts, he tells her. He details each one in a litany of lust. This is exactly the kind of love relationship with God we sing about in chapel—an eternity of staring.

The time-bound, real-world alternative that Marvell's speaker proposes to his love—in case you're wondering what happens next in this racy poem—captures more of the spirit of my relationship with God. Hearing "Time's winged chariot" coming up behind him, he urges his love to hurry up and consummate their love—that is, to "roll all our strength and all / Our sweetness up into one ball, / And tear our pleasures with rough strife / Through the iron gates of life." Roll. Tear. Rough strife. While some older hymns confess to hearts "prone to wander" and leave the God we love, most of our contemporary chapel songs mention nothing of this manner of love wrestling I have with God and offer none of the hard questions and paradoxical answers I find in almost every Bible passage. No, in the longings of Christians today, I hear cozy firesides, gazing at each other, asking no questions at all. It's all about a fingers of light parting the clouds sort of a relationship, just like the one Charlotte wishes would last forever.

Not that I would have anything against enjoying God myself in that way. I know the words of the songs I just quoted because I love to sing them, and I share my students' and my daughter's desire to connect with God as intimately as with a lover—however scary that concept might be. I, too, long to see and hear and be "loved on"—as my children used to call their morning hugging sessions on my lap—by my father in heaven. And occasionally I can almost sense God's presence in that way too—when I'm picking blackberries in summer, for example, and suddenly notice that I am surrounded by his bounty.

It's just that my own experience of getting to know him has been more about moving toward him—and often away from him—through conflict and questioning and struggle. Deep down, I don't believe growth happens—any growth, not just spiritual growth—without sinews being stretched and backs being bent and shoes getting too small. Charlotte started developing breasts and pubic hair when she was still in elementary school. If she didn't struggle with this evidence of growth, I know I did, and still am.

And the worst of it, friends with older children tell me, is yet to come. That's growth. Changing. Metamorphosing in one's most private places. Wanting to stay the same while at the same time wanting to leave it all behind you. Struggling.

The life story of just about every faith hero of scripture, it seems to me, validates my experience as a struggler. Through doubting and running from God and striving against him, the faithful grow in knowledge of and belief in God, and their slowly increasing faith, like Abraham's, is credited to them as righteousness.

In Isaiah, the Lord offers a picture of what growing in faith in his presence looks like. "Though you do not acknowledge me," he promises his anointed, nevertheless,

> I will go before you
> and will level the mountains;
> I will break down gates of bronze
> and cut through bars of iron.
> I will give you the treasures of darkness,
> riches stored in secret places,
> so that you may know that I am the LORD,
> the God of Israel, who summons you by name. (Isaiah 45:2–3)

Being in God's presence is all about following after him through destruction and turmoil and discovering his treasures in the secrecy and darkness of our struggling hearts. For Charlotte, God be thanked, such times are still unthinkable, even as God recedes, out of her sight, into the unknown behind the clouds.

Relevant and cited scriptural passages: Genesis 32:22–32, Job, Jonah, Isaiah 45:2–3, and Hebrews 11.

Other references:

Keith Green. "Oh Lord, You're Beautiful." Pretty Good Records. 1980.

Dennis Jernigan. "If I Could Just Sit With You Awhile." Shepherd's Heart Music. 1992.

Andrew Marvell. "To His Coy Mistress." 1681.

Robert Robinson. "Come Thou Fount of Every Blessing." 1758.

10

*The Treasures
of Darkness, Part 2*

My profession, the teaching of English, is all about struggle. Every novel or play or short story we call literature is, at its essence, a conflict. However postmodern we may be, we still buy into the classical structure of fictional works that requires, before all else, something bad happening before anything good can come of it. Characters suffer and grow in all great literature. Indeed, we call them flat characters and question a literary work's quality if they do not. A story is rising and falling action, conflict then resolution, struggle resulting in growth. There is no story without conflict, I tell would-be story writers. Universal truth is ratified, in literature as in life, not through a character's mere mindless affirmations of it but through the lifelong study that comes from doubting and challenging and searching and returning to the problem again and again.

And not only the characters but we ourselves grow through the study of literature. The other day I read a short story by Beth Lordan called "Penumbra" in the *Atlantic Monthly*. In it, a man who is dying of cancer goes to Ireland with his wife, fulfilling a lifelong dream of theirs. Once there, all he wants to do is go back home and die, and his wife, although terribly disappointed, makes the arrangements to abort the trip. In a particularly horrible scene, on their last day in Ireland, the dying man tries to express his gratitude to his wife for understanding his situation and giving up their dream. But what comes out of his mouth instead is a confession about all the fantasies he's had about other women throughout their marriage. Although the subject matter is bleak, and this truly terrible event occurs in it, the story offers a sort of redemption at the end, or what must pass for redemption for a man nearing death with no expectation of a life beyond this one. After his idiotic confession, he gets lost and needs to go to the bathroom and, upon entering an abandoned hut on the beach, experiences an illusion of "being suspended among stars." Back at the hotel, his wife, hurt and angry, has gone to a bar, but he finds her and brings the scarf she needs against the cold, and, at the very end of the story, their hands touch. I read the story all in one sitting after coming home from work, while the spaghetti sauce simmered on the stove and my daughters tried to get a cow out in the field to eat some grass they picked for her rather than the grass that she was tearing off with her own yellow teeth.

Later that night, after my children were in bed and their nighttime rituals—reading for awhile, being loved on in their beds, adjusting the bedroom door to be just the right amount of open and closed—had been completed and after my husband and I had read awhile and turned out the light, I found myself crying.

I thought it was about me. My husband did too. That afternoon the therapist I've been working with had questioned me about some of the underlying sources of the fears and rages that grip me, and we ended the session with the plan to start talking about my childhood problems and other hard things the next week. Now my husband, holding me and feeling my crying, tried to comfort me.

"You don't have to talk about any of that," he told me. "Just don't." And I thought about the comfort he offered, that maybe I should just put off talking about such painful subjects for now, or forever. I knew that I wouldn't avoid them, though, that I would go there, to that place I had left behind, go to whatever past horror I had to in order to escape present or future ones.

Even later, though, after my husband's breathing got longer and thicker and I had drifted off then wakened again to the unearthly piping of coyotes in the woods, I realized it wasn't for me that I was crying but for the man in the story, a man whose name I couldn't even remember, a man who didn't even exist except as ink on a few pages recounting a series of made-up events, surprising and horrible but somehow familiar, in my mind. I cried that the man was going to die, that his attempt to express love turned into hurting the very one he loved, that he—like so many others—had no better comfort in this life than the brush of a hand against a hand, no more compelling promise for the future than a vision of himself floating in a swirl of stars. In the secret of night, I mourned the fate of the lost and the difficulty of loving others as myself. Through reading literature, you see, I coexperience others' struggles and occasional joys. Great literature grows me.

My own focus in the study of English is on the other end—the writing end. Here the role of struggle is even more apparent, as I'm sure you know if you've ever written anything you intended others to read. To write at all is to wrestle the ideas and images in one's head onto the page and thus find some relief from them. To write for others is to re-create the very conflicts—of confusion and hope and the secret fear that you might be wrong—that you are trying to escape.

I am currently rereading the key works of an author whose writing I loved in my undergraduate years, D. H. Lawrence. The main character of his early novel *Sons and Lovers* refers to one of the women he loves, a deep-eyed believer who knows him better than any other, as "the threshing-floor on which he threshed out all his beliefs. While he trampled his ideas upon her soul, the truth came out for him." The metaphor exactly expresses the role that writing plays in my own pursuit of truth: it is the threshing-floor on which I tramp out all my ideas and seek God in them. *Thresh* means to beat or flail, my dictionary says, to separate the grain from the straw, an act as synonymously violent as its variant *thrash*. And yet, if one is hungry and hasn't a combine handy, there is no other way.

Playwright Thornton Wilder once said, "I've never forgotten for long at a time that living is struggle. I know that every good and excellent thing in the world stands moment by moment on the razor-edge of danger and must be fought for—whether it's a field, or a home, or a country." Or God, I would add. The interface of my faith and my field of study, I would say, is struggle, as is every area of my life in which I grow and change and get now closer to, now further from, the object of my most overwhelming desire: to be back home with the one who made me and loved me enough to hold me, squirming, to himself. How can we as believers do anything but struggle, I wonder, given that we are made in the image of our Creator and are yet so essentially—at our very core as sinful creatures—unlike him?

Not long after I started teaching at the Christian university where I still teach, I was recruited to a committee called the Spiritual Formation Task Force, made up of two professors of biblical studies, the campus pastor, the director of student ministries, and the head of student development—all lifelong Christians and also experts in the development (psychological and spiritual) of students. Having only been a Christian myself for a few years, I was more useful as a case study in spiritual formation than as a source of knowledge in such matters. And, never having had even an introductory psychology class, I didn't know anything at all about the developmental phases that were the foundation of much of the scholarship in this area. Nevertheless, what we talked about paralleled everything I knew from blind experience: that students grew spiritually through their struggles. Every once in a while we would get sidetracked into the spiritual disciplines or fight about the finer theological details of sanctification, but the one characteristic of spiritual growth about which we all agreed—because we all knew it to be true from our own stormy pasts—was that spiritual growth derives directly from spiritual crisis. This equation is so true that it works conversely: without significant suffering, there is no growth.

After a year or two of meeting and discussing, we came up with a mission statement and some strategies for implementing it: retreats and chapel topics and various programs. Then the group more or less disbanded. I guess it was a good thing for me, this task force. I learned a lot. But the meetings and our endless programming left me, finally, dissatisfied, because if there was one thing I thought should have come of it all, it was that we should tell our students the one truth that we had agreed upon, a truth that belied the very programs that we came up with: growth, spiritual or otherwise, could not be planned. No retreat or chapel presentation could cause it. In order to grow—in their relationships with God and one another as well as in their studies and as individuals—our students would have to struggle with God and one another, with their parents, with us, and with themselves. They would have to ask hard questions—what they were studying and why, who God is and what is true, what our purpose is as Christians and how to live in this world—and they should never be satisfied with pat answers.

"What are we going to do?" someone on the Spiritual Formation Task Force joked when I suggested that we throw out what we had worked on and start back at the beginning. "Tell them to go out and have a spiritual crisis?"

And, in truth, I figure God himself has a spiritual formation plan for each of us. To each of his children, he whispers this wonderful, awful promise:

> I will give you the treasures of darkness,
> riches stored in secret places,
> so that you may know that I am the LORD,
> the God of Israel, who summons you by name. (Isaiah 45:3)

Someday I may tell my daughters the truth about getting closer to God. More likely I will pray it on their behalf in my writing. For now, though, I encourage them to read books, tell stories, play with the cows, and enjoy it when the sun is high in a sky full of puffy clouds. Their crises, I figure, will come.

Relevant and cited scriptural passages: Isaiah 45:3.
Other references:
D. H. Lawrence. *Sons and Lovers*. 1913.
Beth Lordan. "Penumbra: A Short Story." *Atlantic Monthly*. February 2002, p. 77.
Thornton Wilder. *The Skin of Our Teeth*. 1942.

11

Stairs

I began the new year with a plan—I'm afraid to call it a resolution or it will inevitably fail—to work out more often than I
did last semester. That is, to work out at all. So far I've been
to the University Health Center twice. I've chosen the stair-stepper machine as my way to less flab and less grouchiness for one
reason: it's the only machine that has a little ledge on which to put
a book so you can read while you exercise. I'm reading a book I
got out of the library called *Texts of Terror*, by Phyllis Trible.

"Why do you read stuff like that?" Lulu asked me when she saw
it on the breakfast table the other morning.

By "stuff like that" I suppose she means books about unpleasant things like violence and suffering, like the last specimen of my
morning reading that her big sister, Charlotte, had noticed and
commented upon, a book called *Trauma and Recovery*.

"This sure looks boring," was her child's assessment of the
book's plain cover and incomprehensible title.

"What's trauma?" Charlotte wanted to know, pronouncing the
word trow-ma. "What's recovery?" I explained each word: when a

really bad thing happens to you, when you get over something, like an illness. Even though Charlotte just won the elementary spelling bee and knows how to spell words like *turophile*, *preprandial*, and *exegesis*, she doesn't know these words, and I am glad. I hope she never will.

The stair-stepper machine was complicated to maneuver at first. You have to select a program—fat burner, aerobic training, rapid running—then enter your weight, the degree of intensity of the training you want to do, and how long you want to do it. Of course, none of the exercise programs you can choose make sense unless you have already tried them. And none that I have discovered so far achieve what I really want: an effortless, pain-free, and even entertaining melting away of fat and tension, like what the exercise equipment infomercials advertise on TV. Skinny girls grinning away as though they're not only *not* suffering but enjoying what they're doing.

The first time I used the machine, I chose steady climb, which was okay, but I had to keep switching the levels up and down. The warm-up planned for a fat person like me was way too slow, and I was sure that all the students pumping away around me were looking over and mentally clucking their tongues at the pathetic middle-aged professor trying in vain to get in shape. When the warm-up was over, though, I had to grope crazily for the down arrows to avoid the heart attack the warning label on the machine said was imminent.

This time, I punch in the random program and leave it on the fat-person setting. I checked out *Texts of Terror* weeks earlier but have not yet found time to sit down and enjoy it. It's about, as I told Lulu, the scary parts of the Bible, where people do really bad things to one another. It's also about how, as Christians, we're supposed to deal with the fact that people routinely referred to as "men of faith" in the Bible, even in the New Testament, committed amazing acts of violence against others and hardly seemed to be called to account. Often the victims of these violent acts were women, but, despite their endurance of evil done to them, we never refer to them as martyrs or even "*women* of faith."

I didn't tell Lulu that last part, because before I did she interrupted me with the usual questions. What scary stories? What people? What really bad things? And while I searched around in my head for a really bad story from the Bible that was not quite so scary as the rape of a sister, the dismemberment of a concubine, a man's murder of his daughter when she runs out to welcome him home after a battle, or another man's offer of his virgin daughters to the rapists outside so they will stop insisting on having sex with his male visitors, I thought, *Thank you thank you thank you God that she doesn't yet know these things, that she can't yet imagine such happenings, that she, like her older sister, doesn't really understand even the vocabulary of violence and suffering.*

What I wanted to find out from *Texts of Terror* was the answer to some of my own questions about the story of Amnon and Absalom and their sister Tamar and father David, the "royal rape" as Trible calls it. Why is Amnon filled with hate toward the object of his "love" as soon as he rapes her, as so often happens with rapists, who often then go on to maim or kill their victims? What exactly *is* this connection between love and hate? And why did Absalom not immediately and openly report his brother's act of violence and dishonor? Why did he not confront Amnon and call on his father and mother and the rest of the community to do the same? Why did David, the dad of all this mess, do nothing when he found out about it? And if Amnon's friend, Jonadab, picked up on something being not quite right with the crown prince's feelings for his beautiful sister, then surely Amnon's dad, King David, must have noticed something, too. Could David have even knowingly sent his own daughter in to her lusting half-brother? Tamar herself seems to suggest as much when she points out that her father would certainly "not withhold" her from Amnon if he would pursue her in a more legitimate manner.

And what happened to Tamar after her retreat to Absalom's house? Did she waste away and die a dishonored woman? Did she develop post-traumatic stress disorder, as I did following a much less traumatic encounter with sexual violence? Or could she have become one of Absalom's paramours? Both were famously good-looking, and Absalom later names one of his daughters after her, a daughter whose name we learn even though we never learn the name of the child's mother. And Absalom eventually ends up committing fratricide and arson and so on, so it's not like he's any more of a paragon of honorable behavior than his dad was.

I was never actually raped, in case you're worried I'll start going on about it. I was never the victim of incest. Relax. I will not upset you with an account of such horrors. I was merely held up in a phone booth at gunpoint many years ago, when I was about the age of my students, and very minimally sexually assaulted. A hand in my clothes. Words. That's all.

But still I have these questions about violence. Having become a Christian many years after my own assault, I am especially interested in what the Bible has to say about such matters and how to reconcile that with what it says by omission by presenting accounts of such atrocities without much comment, without criticism, with nothing but the glib historical glosses of my *NIV Study Bible* commentators to help me to understand what I might be intended to learn from them. I need to figure this out, you see, because even now, twenty years after an event much less atrocious than any of the ones I've been reading about in the Bible, I flip out and get sick whenever bad things happen, like September 11th or the Oklahoma City bombing or even when an especially aggressive student gets really mad about a grade or verbally attacks another student in my class. I need to understand the event of which these responses are a legacy. I need to let the pain of it grow me.

The slim little hardcover library book won't fit on the shelf after all. It is tightly bound and keeps wanting to close up and fall off as I read, so I have to spread my hand out on the pages to keep it open. The little shelf is high above me, at about the right height for a male basketball player to be reading *Texts of Terror*, and I finally give up on the shelf and hold the book in my hands, panting as the stairs and Trible's terse sentences make me go now faster, now slower, now almost stopping, now running hard, as if trying to escape from something too awful for words.

It took me a while to even find a book that addressed the nasty parts of the Bible. You'd think, in our violence and sex rocked culture, there'd be hundreds of books about Amnon and Tamar and Lot and his daughters and the dismemberment of biblical prostitutes in the library of a Christian university. Not so. Here, as always with tales of terror, especially sexual terror, no one wants to look at them or talk about them or acknowledge them or do anything about them.

I listen to Dr. Laura on the radio when I can, not because of her advice to people morally at sea so much as to hear her callers, almost always people with victims of rage and violence and pain in their lives. The victims themselves rarely call. They have long since given up trying to make anyone hear their stories, much less understand them. Rather, it is the family and friends of victims who call with their questions. Should I marry a man who wants nothing to do with my children from a previous marriage? Should I forgive the man who murdered my teenage daughter? Should I let my husband's children ostracize my own child? Should my sister invite the man who fondled my niece to her own marriage ceremony? Should I attend if she does? And so on.

Thankfully, Dr. Laura's answer to such callers, often drawn from the Old Testament texts she reveres as a practicing Jew, is always no. No, you should *not* victimize children. You are *not* to countenance the victimization of others. You must *not* celebrate with those who rape, murder, and hurt others. You are *not* called, *not* in the Torah or even the New Testament, to forgive those who commit such acts unless they ask you to and genuinely express remorse. No, no, no, of course, no. But what fascinates me, what horrifies me, is not the harsh *no* of Dr. Laura's answer or her unusual reading of Jewish and Christian law but the bizarre impulse that drives these callers to ask their questions. How can I smooth this over? Shouldn't we just put it behind us? The question that lurks beneath their questions is always: How can I make this ugly event fit into the effortless, pain-free life I want to be living?

When I get to the passages about those responsible for Tamar's well-being—her other brother, her father, her community—the stair-stepper plateaus suddenly on the seven notch, and I have to work hard to keep up. The relationships are confusing. Tamar is first referred to as only Absalom's sister, but then Amnon is Absalom's brother. So, I'm thinking, okay, Tamar and Absalom have the same mom, but not Amnon, and Amnon and Absalom are nevertheless seen as brothers because of lineage and inheritance issues, especially in the context of their royal blood. But then, later in the story,

Amnon's crafty friend Jonadab refers to Tamar as Amnon's sister, and Jonadab himself is David's brother's son, which makes him a cousin to the siblings, and everyone's related somehow, and I'm lost. Aren't families supposed to take care of one another? Sweat drips into my eyes and onto the pages of the book. I can't read very well at this pace, so I imagine the members of Tamar's family calling Dr. Laura.

"Should I attend my sister's wedding to this man who used to be my brother's best friend? Actually, he was his cousin, or our cousin, I guess. You see, he helped my brother rape my sister, or anyway that's what some of my family say, and, well, my brother's been dead for awhile now, murdered by another brother of mine, and everyone's kind of forgotten about what's happened, and I don't want to stir anything up, but I just can't see myself being there where he is. I mean, what if he really did help arrange the rape? Doesn't that make him an accomplice or something? And anyway, I've never really liked him because one time he said my sister was a slut, and, I'm like, *this* is the girl he's about to marry! . . ."

The stair-stepper slows, and I check the time, and it's only a minute and thirty-nine seconds until my twenty-five minutes is over. I close the book and set it up on the shelf and concentrate on slowing down. I breathe deeply, the way they tell you to do when you're in a panic, then let out all the air before taking another long breath. When the machine finally stops altogether, it lists what I've achieved: 141 kilowatts, 139 calories, 56 flights of stairs in twenty-five minutes. *About half the flights of stairs there would have been in the World Trade Center towers*, I think to myself. *Not nearly enough if I had been near the top.*

Relevant and cited scriptural passages: Genesis 19, Judges 11 and 19, 2 Samuel 13, and Hebrews 11:32–40.

Other references:

Judith Herman. *Trauma and Recovery: The Aftermath of Violence—from Domestic Abuse to Political Terror*. NY. Basic. 1992.

Phyllis Trible. *Texts of Terror: Literary-Feminist Readings of Biblical Narratives*. Philadelphia: Fortress, 1984.

12

On Responding to Pain

At my daughters' soccer games, when a kid gets hurt on the field, all the other players on both teams "take a knee" while the coaches (and sometimes the mom or dad of the kid) figure out if the injury is serious. If it is, the kid is taken off the field, and everyone claps. I always cry during all this—the taking of the knee, the wondering if the kid is okay, the clapping. If either of my daughters is nearby, I have to duck my head to keep from embarrassing them.

Girls new to the league have to be told what to do when someone gets hurt. Although I'm not the most engaged soccer mom when it comes to knowing what's happening on the field and have even found myself accidentally rooting for the wrong team, if I notice a girl still standing when a player is down, I shout with her teammates, "Take a knee! Take a knee!" until the confused little girl figures it out enough to follow their lead.

Every season, in the midst of the stress of our two girls' games and practices taking up nearly every evening of the week, my husband and I fight it out about whether or not to let them continue.

My husband trots out all the benefits of soccer—learning to play with other kids, working as a team, getting exercise.

"But we never eat at home anymore," I argue. "And the girls stay up too late and are too worn out to do their chores or practice piano."

But then, in my mind, I see the solemn faces and mud-smudged knees. I hear their urgent little voices in the silence of interrupted play, "Take a knee! Take a knee!" And I think, maybe one more season.

In short, if it weren't for this business of taking a knee, none of the boons of playing soccer would be worth the loss of family time and the girls' plain old playtime, time to do nothing at all. So powerful is the image of taking a knee for me that I have unconsciously adopted the practice in my head and now join those kneeling girls in my mind whenever I see someone down or hear about some atrocity in the news, mentally taking a knee for victims, although they don't know it.

Taking a moment to be reverent toward someone else's pain, I have been learning, provides me with the mental clarity I need to respond appropriately to it. My first honest responses, I hate to admit, are likely to be wrong, all wrong—despite the fact that, having once been a victim of violent crime, I know firsthand how even the most well-meaning responses to someone's else's pain often compound it. Many details of the assault were muddled in my mind right after it happened, and I couldn't remember my attackers well enough to identify them meaningfully or pick their photos from hundreds of others that the police later showed me. But to this day I can recall every word of what people said to me in the aftermath of the crime. Every kind-hearted remark in my pain-twisted mind was another attack, blaming *me*, the victim, for what had happened.

"You shouldn't have been making a call from a public phone booth in the middle of the night," one of the two police officers who arrived on the scene told me. When I recounted my story for them to document in their report, the other officer observed that, since there wasn't technical penetration, the sexual assault itself wasn't worth recording. The assailant, if caught, would have to do a lot more time for using a weapon to rob me. He wrote down only the armed robbery of the contents of my purse: three dollars and some pricy sunglasses. Both officers were white and made racist comments about my assailants, the same exact comments that my black neighbors made when I finally got up the courage to return to my apartment a few weeks later.

Confronting my ensuing depression, my friends told me, "You should be so happy to be alive." Perhaps I should have been, but I wished I were dead for a long time after the assault.

The boyfriend I had been on the phone with at the time of the assault never once mentioned it to me afterwards. My father also refused to discuss what had happened and coached my siblings not to discuss it either because, he told them, "It'll just upset her."

In the two English courses I was teaching at the time, I cried in front of my students, whose papers and final exams and course records my assailants took with them. But my students ignored my distress and told me angrily it wasn't fair that they had to hand back in the work they had done earlier in the semester in order to get a grade in the class.

My attackers also took my own papers for my three graduate courses. This all happened back in the days of typewriters and, if you were a careful sort of person (which I wasn't), carbon copies. One of my professors didn't believe me that I had been held up and wanted the fifty-page paper by its original due date at the end of the week. The second professor looked peeved and gave me an extension till after Christmas. The third, an ancient professor emeritus still teaching by popular demand, was the only person in all my acquaintance who responded in a way that helped me: he was amazed and distraught at my tearful account and even cried himself, and he did not want me to worry about my final paper in his course. "You were getting an A, anyway," he said.

Decades later, the assault still haunts me, and I relive it whenever I experience, directly or vicariously, an attack out of the blue. When a high school student I taught some years ago became violent in class, I fell apart in the classroom. Later, at the college where I now teach, a young man verbally attacked a young woman in my classroom, and I went into first a rage, then a crippling panic attack that lasted for weeks. When the Murrah Building in Oklahoma City was blown up and hundreds were killed, I sank into an angry ugly depression, and with the attack on the World Trade Center, I developed symptoms of full-blown post-traumatic stress disorder: I couldn't sleep, jumped at the slightest noise, didn't want to be touched by my husband or even my little daughters, was consumed by rage or terror all the time, couldn't drive or grade papers or do anything that required intense focus, and alternately couldn't eat or ate all the time.

People's responses to my pain—the negative ones and the loving one—have profoundly affected my life since the assault. Some weeks after September 11th, I had a revelation of just how this happens. My family and I were on our way home from church. It was the first time I had attended church since the attack. I had quit going to church because I was maniacally certain that our pastor, who was preaching a series on spiritual gifts at the time, would not talk about the attack and its spiritual ramifications but would stick to his scheduled topic, which hardly seemed relevant under the circumstances. In fact this didn't happen. He preached about nothing but the attack during the weeks I wasn't there and only resumed the spiritual gifts series upon my return. Oh well.

I was in despair during those weeks. I needed people. Friends and family—my husband, my daughters, my sister, my father. My colleagues. My students. The members of my church. I needed their love and understanding, their non-judgmental attention and shared grief. The problem was, as in the days after the phone booth attack, I didn't know how to ask for these comforts, and nobody seemed to know how to give them.

I didn't help them. I was difficult to approach, angry and distant and desirous of space. My daughters couldn't understand what was happening, why I didn't want them to come sit on my lap every morning as they always did upon getting up, why I spoke shortly to them and didn't pay any attention to their questions. My husband didn't really understand my behavior either, but both of us had by then figured out enough to connect the Twin Tower attack to my phone booth experience. So, on this Sunday, he was trying to explain what he knew to the girls.

"Mama is sick," he told them. "She has been sick for about a month now. That's why she's always mad or crying." He hesitated. It's hard to explain mental health and sexual assaults to children, after all. Even adults don't like talking about such matters.

"But why is Mama sick?" they wanted to know.

"Well," he said, "she says it's because of the September 11th attack, but I think she's just working too hard."

That apparently satisfied my daughters, and, as soon as we got home, I went for a walk through the woods to try and work off my anger towards this man who loved me. *She says. Just working too hard. My fault.* If I'd just stop working so hard, he seemed to say, I wouldn't have this problem. The phone booth would go away. I stomped through the woods, shattering the brown leaves and little twigs under my feet.

"I married the wrong person," I told my husband when I got back. "I should have married that old man who cried when I told him I had been attacked, and instead I married the policeman who blamed me for it. I shouldn't have been making a phone call in the middle of the night. I shouldn't have been coming home from the library on my bike at midnight. I shouldn't be working so hard now."

I did not plan these words. As soon as I said them, I saw as in a vision this picture of how my mind works: I put all responses to my pain, either real ones like my husband's or predicted ones like what the pastor of my church would preach over, through what I saw as a shape sorter, one of those box-shaped baby toys with different shaped holes to put different shaped blocks through. I sorted others' responses to my pain into the responses I knew from the past— reproach, refusal to talk about it, deflection, minimalization, irritation, rage, disgust. Except for one old man, whom I only knew at the time of the assault as a voice lecturing on Shakespeare far away at the front of a large classroom, no one knew how to comfort me. Many blamed me. Most leapt to conclusions about what had happened. Key people—my father, my boyfriend—never said a word to me about it at all, and most of my friends were discernibly irritated or embarrassed when I said anything about the assault. Why was I still harping on it, their impatience seemed to demand. They remarked that I was no fun to be with anymore. No one paid attention to the news stories that incapacitated me. No one cried.

Recently, an old friend in Boston told me she was being harassed by an ex-boyfriend, a guy I had never met before but knew from previous accounts had always been alarmingly possessive. Years ago, I had said something to that effect, something about the alarm, and it irked her. She had met the guy at church, she said—as though that precluded any possibility of imperfection on his part, much less danger to her—and she wouldn't listen to any criticism. Now, over a year after they had broken up, he was following her everywhere all of a sudden and jamming her phone machine with messages whenever she was away from home for longer than an hour or two. She had changed her phone number twice, but they had a lot of friends in common, and somehow he managed to find out each new number. She was thinking about quitting her job and moving away. Perhaps to New York, she said. Or maybe out my way even—she was that panicked. Only her faith was keeping her going, she told me. Finally, just the day before, in desperation, she had e-mailed him, hoping he would see what he was doing and, through seeing it, return to God. That was her prayer. Out of a jumble of friends and acquaintances from my past, her voice on the phone became a person in pain, but my immediate response was to judge her motives. *Why was she telling me this? Why wasn't she going to the police? Why was she e-mailing this creep? Could she secretly be wanting to continue the connection?*

I felt bad for her, but what made it into my immediate response was an exhortation that she see a therapist and get some help. I didn't overtly say it, but my underlying message was this: You are to blame for this situation—writing the e-mail, not going to the police, not handling things as I would—and a therapist will make you see it. Worse, although I had been quick to read her boyfriend as a bad guy in the past, in that moment I was all but blind to the actual aggressor in her story: a man who, regardless of her response, was pursuing her against her wishes and causing her to live a life of pain. Her voice went flat, losing all the jagged plaintiveness of confession and entreaty, and afterwards she didn't want to talk about the ex-boyfriend anymore. We never spoke of him again. I am now a sharp-edged triangle in her shape sorter, or a needle-pointed star. I botched my one chance to offer comfort, and there is no fixing it.

I am not writing this to gain sympathy from you, or in penance for my own misdeeds, but rather to help you and myself know how to comfort others in pain. Comforting others is not an easy task. Perhaps it truly is a spiritual gift and cannot be taught or learned. For many, like me and many of those who love me, it is certainly counterintuitive.

Only children, in my experience, really understand how comfort works. Intuitively they seek it, when hurt. A kiss, to a child, actually heals a scraped knee. Children shamelessly enjoy being comforted. When Charlotte was a toddler, she would duck her forehead to the floor pretending to hurt herself just so that I would swoop down on her and kiss the hurt place and make it better.

A child's commiseration is real. My daughters have written me love letters and made me presents when I was in bed with the flu. When they were younger, they used to cry when I cried, but as they get older, it embarrasses them and makes them mad. "Don't cry," they warn me sternly when we get to the sad part of a movie or book. Or at those soccer games when a child is hurt.

Grown-ups, however, at least in our culture, have forgotten how to mourn. Either that or they just avoid mourning altogether. Fewer and fewer people have actual funeral services for their loved ones these days, it seems to me. And, if they do, they often substitute good behaviors—such as donating money to a cause—for the few remaining mourning traditions our culture still has, such as buying flowers or making food for the mourning family.

When I read the book of Lamentations in the Bible, I am struck by the sheer strangeness of such a document, which seems to have no other purpose than to mourn. This is the book that Jews read aloud to this day at the Wailing Wall in Jerusalem. The book offers a litany of evils—slavery, war, exile, the destruction of cities, and starvation so severe it drives mothers to "eat their offspring." But in place of the censure one might expect, the biblical writer responds to each new evil with the purest sorrow, unadulterated by a wagging finger or stern reminders or even the faintest I-told-you-so:

My eyes fail from weeping,
I am in torment within,
my heart is poured out on the ground
because my people are destroyed
because children and infants faint in the streets of the city. (2:11)

Over and over again the speaker recounts his sadness:

Streams of tears flow from my eyes
because my people are destroyed.
My eyes will flow unceasingly,
without relief,
until the LORD looks down
from heaven and sees. (3:48–50)

The speaker's only complaint is that others don't share his pain: "Is it nothing to you, all of you who pass by?" he asks (1:12). As is the case so often in our culture, the writer notes that "People have heard my groaning, but there is no one to comfort me" (1:21). Still, this voice sounds so foreign. It seems to me that I and most of the people I know have forgotten how to grieve like this—not only for others but for ourselves. We have forgotten how to grieve at all. It no longer comes naturally to us. We have to learn it from self-help books and therapists. Or we have to do without.

All I have to offer you is a list of don'ts. Don't forbid painful topics. Don't judge. Don't preach. When people tell you of their pain, don't say anything at all. Don't think, if you can help it, at least at first. Just hear it and, if you can, cry. Cry for them and for yourself, because you, too, have suffered such things, or will. Cry that there is evil in this world, that we are all of us sometimes the victims and often the perpetrators of it. Cry that people, however messed up, and even if they themselves caused the misery in which they find themselves, have to suffer at all, and that many, because they have forgotten even how to seek comfort in their pain, will never find it and will suffer forever. Remind yourself of these truths about the pain of our world and the sins that occasion it. Others' sins. Our own sins. Because it is only this grieving, this taking of a knee, that truly comforts us, that connects us to one another and to God.

Relevant and cited scriptural passages: Lamentations 2:11 and 3:48–50.

13

Servanthood

The last words I remember saying one morning before stomping out the door and driving on to work were, "I am not your servant." I was speaking to Charlotte, who was maybe nine at the time. I settled the plate of eggs with ham and onions and the cup of Earl Grey tea—with one-fourth teaspoon of milk and three tablespoons of sugar—on the rickety TV table in front of her: the breakfast she had ordered, after fifteen full minutes of making up her mind.

Charlotte always has trouble making up her mind if there's any kind of pressure. The pressure, in this case, was that it was a typical school morning, a Wednesday, as it happened, and Wednesday mornings are one of the times, precious to me, that I set aside to go to the Bagel Café near my university and grade papers. Charlotte, of course, knew this. I may have reminded her of it. In any case, *I* knew it. I treasured every second of the uncommon two and one half hours of what I call my alone time, time so unusual in my life that it has the supernatural power of turning whatever I do then, even grading papers, into deep pleasure. At the Bagel Café, I don't even need to order my tea. The staff automatically sets out the giant cup I prefer, one of their *café au lait* cups, and fills it right to the top and sticks in a plastic spoon so I can get the tea bag out when it has brewed to the color of transparent leather. No one talks to me. I drink my tea and read paper after paper. It seems to me I can get twice as many papers graded then as at any other time.

To prod my daughter along, I had had to run down the short list of possible Charlotte breakfasts. Eggs with ham and onions. Cheerios with NOT TOO MUCH milk. Toast, but only if it remained crunchy after being slathered with butter, a physical impossibility unless you are my mother-in-law. Bacon made not in a frying pan but in the microwave (another specialty of my mother-in-law). I sighed loudly several times. Charlotte protested that she couldn't make up her mind if I hurried her, and her upper lip twisted into the U-shape it gets whenever she's about to cry.

I could feel my husband's presence behind me, willing me to patience. The morning before, after I had left, Charlotte had had a time-pressure mad fit before he finally got them off to school, and I knew he didn't want her to have another one. Now, offhandedly, Charlotte chose her breakfast, and I immediately went about chopping a thin slice of onion, then two slices of the turkey lunch-meat my children call ham, meanwhile microwaving the water for her tea. By the time I got the egg out of the refrigerator, Lulu, who has a history of digestive difficulties and is currently going through an ominous phase of not eating breakfast, had emerged from her room and was asking, "What's that smell?" I had burned the onions. I started over. Twenty minutes of my two and one half hours ticked away. Thirty minutes of rest and bliss, lost forever.

I pushed the door to the TV room open with my toe and set-tled the plate and the cup in front of Charlotte. She moved her head impatiently around me to see some detail from a scene in *Invisible Dad*, the movie she and Lulu had rented that week and were now watching for the fifth or sixth time.

"I am not your servant," I told the side of her head, my words muffled by anger louder than noise, by anger that I knew would curve the lip again and bring the tears that had threatened thirty-seven minutes earlier, tears that would render the breakfast suddenly unwanted and inedible, tears that would accompany me like an illness the whole day, tingeing everything I did—even grading papers in the Bagel Café—with the overwhelming desire to sleep or leave wherever I was or in some way escape my body, to burst open like a cicada and fly up out of the brown, hard husk of myself into the open sky.

On the drive to work, I thought about servanthood. Commands. No *please*. No *thank you*. The uneaten eggs, framed by a film of solidified butter, cold and hard on the plate when I got home. And, worst of all, the loss of my magical alone time—because now, I reasoned crankily, it was ruined, hardly an hour, and tainted by my own guilt and meanness. I couldn't see myself in that place, at my little uneven table in the back room of the Bagel Café where the light is the best, surrounded by folders of my students' work, at peace.

I have recently been lamenting that, having come late to Christianity and missed out on Awana and the habit of memorizing scripture, I cannot recall a single passage from the Bible on demand. Nevertheless, a verse inhabited me as I drove. I can think of no other way to explain its sudden presence in my mind. A Bible verse, confidently intact, from some accidental storage place in my brain. Or from God himself—there's always that possibility. Jesus said, "If anyone wants to be first, he must be the very last, the servant of all" (Mark 9:35). I stewed and I drove and I tried to ignore the words.

Occasionally I get solace from Jesus' words, but more often, as in this instance, I find him flat-out irritating. I must seek to be commanded, the words interpreted themselves from out of the broth of my anger and guilt and refusal to listen. I must seek to be commanded by my very own children. I must do without *please* or *thanks*. I should seek to serve without these incentives—indeed, I should desire it. With what horrible inadequacy as a parent, as a person, was I created that I could not do so?

I have many Christian friends, all of whom have been at this business of living under grace longer than I have, who like to ignore the *shoulds* of the Bible. Several have told me that they're only there to show us our own inadequacies, our need for God's mercy. Others speak of legalism—if you preoccupy yourself with what all you're supposed to do or not do, they tell me, you're a legalist, which is worse than being a sinner, from what I gather. They have explained to me that our inability to do what's expected of us is forgiven, all forgiven, through Christ's death. And they say that the counsel on right living is only there in the text because, upon being saved, we will *want* to know how to do better, we will *desire* to be more like Jesus. I don't, however. Somehow, this miracle hasn't happened to me. Try as I might, I have *no* desire to be a servant.

We are right now approaching my least favorite holiday, Halloween. I call it a holiday—or holy day—because that's what it is in our culture, a day held holy in our schools and families, and, as hard as I have tried, I have found it impossible to wrest it from my family's schedule. When the children were babies, I would simply forget the day and one time had to give the neighbor kids fungus-spotted apples from my mother-in-law's tree because I had no candy or cookies or even shiny coins in the house. When the girls got a little older, we took them to the Harvest Festival of the First Baptist Church, where, they were told in their Sunday school classes beforehand, they could only dress up as characters from the Bible.

"Oh, good," Charlotte told her teacher. "I'm going to be a demon, and demons are in the Bible." Another testimony to my failure as a parent.

This year, Charlotte wants to be an Egyptian. She checked it out with me a few days ago by stretching a stained dishtowel across her forehead and hooking it behind her ears to show me what she meant. When I questioned her further about this—secretly fearful that her desire might be related to a post September 11th demonization of all things Arab prevalent among children at her school—she specified that she needed some striped or otherwise fancy fabric for her costume. "I want to be an Egyptian *princess*," she told me, "not a *servant*."

When I read about being a servant in the Bible, like Charlotte, I get a picture of an undesirable sort of life. Captured by my enemies. Educated for their service. Impregnated by my master so that he can father a son without God's help, then sent away. Imprisoned for not wanting to have sex with the boss's spouse. Always subject to someone else's anger and abuse. Commanded, not asked, as even that kind Roman centurion who wants Jesus to heal his sick servant takes pains to point out.

"I say to my servant, 'Do this,' and he does it," the centurion tells Jesus proudly (Matthew 8:9).

There are some joys of servitude. Being taken care of by my master, if only because I have a definable worth. Learning some intriguing skill now long forgotten—how to thresh grain or make bricks or transport heavy stones great distances without using wheels. Getting to sass back at Peter when he tries to hide himself among the servants huddled around the fire. But largely it seems an unpleasant existence, as impossible to desire as to love people who hate you. But there it is.

"If anyone wants to be first, he must be the very last, and the servant of all," Jesus tells us, and I'm thinking, I do *not* want to be first. Just let me be somewhere in the middle, not first, certainly not last. I sound, I know, just like the mother of those "Sons of Thunder," trying to orchestrate James' and John's places in God's affection. Or like the racist heroine of one of my favorite Flannery O'Connor stories, who wants to rank at least above white trash in the "horde of souls" she imagines "rumbling toward heaven." But I don't care.

And perhaps that's as far as I can get in holy living for today: *I do not want to be first.* Please, Father, who wants to give good things to his children, let me not be first, but just take me, the poor inadequate way I am, and make me yours.

And, if it's not too much trouble, take my daughters, too.

Relevant and cited scriptural passages: Genesis 16 and 39; 2 Kings 5; Daniel 1; Matthew 8:5–13 and 20:20–28; and Mark 3:17, 9:35, and 14:53–72.
Other references:
Flannery O'Connor. "Revelation." *Everything That Rises Must Converge.* New York: Noonday, 1964.

14

Remorse

Remorse is a hard place for me to get to. From the moment I make one of my famous blunt pronouncements or condemning speeches, I am so consumed with the knowledge that I am right and whoever is in disagreement is wrong that there's just no room for second guessing myself. No loophole in my stone tablets of what is true and good to admit even the faint scent of genuine self-critique. Not a chink in my armor of honest opinion through which the most querulous question might slip in. Even when someone bolder than I am steps up and proves me unalterably wrong, as a colleague and friend did at a meeting the other day. Even when, proven wrong, I am roundly punished for my error.

I recently asked a classroom of students to describe the feelings they had had when punished, and they ventured such answers as "convicted" and "guilty" or "like I wished I hadn't done whatever it was." No one offered what I have always felt—that is, righteous anger—although, when I mentioned this response, a couple of them shyly agreed that they had felt that on occasion. And we never did get to the s-word, *shame*, a word rarely used except to accuse others—"You should be ashamed"—and never used in public to describe one's own actions: "I am ashamed." Said aloud, the word unsays itself: "sh-h-h-h-h ame," a shushing, then a falling, followed by silence. What would we say—what is there to say?—if a public figure who had done something wrong, some homicidal dictator or scandalous president or CEO who had destroyed the future of thousands of retiring employees, openly admitted shame?

Well, I am just like them. However often I say the wrong thing or make a bad choice, however miserably I'm punished for my actions, I just can't get there. I always see the right in myself, the good intentions, the truth I sought to force on others. Humble pie, that medieval pastry filled with entrails that now symbolizes voluntary humiliation, is not merely distasteful to me. It is simply not on the menu. Not ever. Although I am a pretty good cook, I don't even know how to make one.

Don't get me wrong. Like you, I often think, after some particularly hellish meeting at which I just had to speak my mind, "Oh, I wish I hadn't said that." But I don't actually repent my words or actions at those times. I rue them.

To rue one's choices is a different thing altogether than to feel remorse. Ruing is about being in a tight spot. Dealing with the comeuppances of one's pride. Wishing—in retrospect—that one had been more politic or secretive in one's attack on others, less open and honest and direct in one's meanness. Even the word itself, to me, has something of the circumspect. To say *rue*, one must grimace and purse one's lips simultaneously, a brownnosing facial expression if there ever was one, a kiss of condemnation. I can easily imagine Judas *ruing* his decision to turn Jesus in to the authorities, although that word is never used in the translations.

Instead, upon recognizing that he stood condemned by his former friends, he "repented" (KJV) his actions or was "sorry" (CEV), "was seized with remorse" (NIV) or simply "changed his mind" (ESV) about keeping the money. The word *rue* shows up in the English language Bible only as a bitter-tasting herb. It is what the Gardener in Shakespeare's *Richard II* plants to mark where the eavesdropping Queen's tears fell. He refers to the plant—snidely, I think—as the "sour herb of grace."

Real remorse is another matter altogether. Remorse is about truly believing oneself to have been wrong—to have been arrogant or selfish or intentionally hurtful in one's proclamations or actions. Remorse is forgetting oneself so extremely as to be able to actually glimpse the world from someone else's point of view, from the point of view of someone less fortunate and more worthy. To consider oneself beneath someone one holds in contempt.

Remorse is the pigpen the prodigal son ends up in—so low that he values the scraps thrown out to feed pigs, creatures lower than the lowest of the low. To eat humble pie and like it. That is remorse, a revelation given to few that leads to the dumbfounded gratefulness of the prodigal son when his father hugs and kisses him and puts a ring on his finger and, as a friend of mine preached in chapel the other day, throws a barbecue in his honor.

I think of how, in their years of servitude, our African slaves revered the offal thrown to them. Pig's intestines and skin and other organs discarded at the Plantation house. Bitter leafed cabbage plants that had long since bolted. The unprocessed grains fed to livestock. They devised recipes for their owners' rubbish and called it the food of the soul, soul food: chitlins, cracklins, collard greens, grits. Of all hymns, the truth-filled spirituals of these same people are among the most powerful testimonies of faith. They even embraced "Amazing Grace," the remorse anthem of a man who had been a slave trader, and called it their own.

Hard though it is for me to imagine a people so abused being themselves motivated by repentance or especially appreciative of unwarranted forgiveness, I think, from their spirituals, they must have been. I cannot think what they did. Perhaps something we might not even consider a crime in the circumstances, some stealing of bread to feed a starving child. Or perhaps something worse than the violence their captors had done to them. Or perhaps the same exact evil—perhaps they themselves had enslaved and abused others they considered less than themselves. Still, from the amazed thankfulness of the songs they sang in more desperate situations than I can imagine, their visions of death as a sweet chariot and Jesus as the grassy bank of a river, I know they repented whatever it was and were joyfully forgiven.

I have suffered from this condition of remorselessness since childhood, and it must be genetic, as my two daughters have apparently inherited it from me or my husband. Probably from both of us. Whenever Kris and I get into an argument, it seems to me he feels no more remorseful about sniping at me than I do at him, at least not until I've worked on him for a while. My daughters, like me but apparently unlike most of my students, react to punishment with outrage. They rarely say they're sorry unless I force them, which I occasionally do just to give them practice with that other s-word that seems to be disappearing from our cultural vocabulary, *sorry*. I am trying to accustom them to the feel of it on the tongue, even though as a sound it lends itself to the most infuriatingly viperous mockery. S-s-s-s-s-s*AWR*-RY! Or, sawrrr-*REE*!

One of the happiest moments of my life as a parent was during Charlotte's eight-year-old tantrum phase—which, by the way, I read in a self-help book was not about manipulation, although I was sure this was wrong, but about her being what the liberal-minded and probably childless idiot who wrote the book referred to as a "spirited child." After various vocal permutations of Proverbs' spare the rod and spoil the child had failed to effect anything but an escalation of Charlotte's tantrums, I had bought the book in desperation.

Spirited children, the author glibly reassured the leftover flower child who was probably the intended audience, were the smartest and best of children. They started throwing tantrums between the ages of seven or eight and twelve not because they were bad or out of control or hopelessly damaged by some screwed up parent like me but because they were just overflowing with spirit. Spirited children couldn't even say what they were mad about when they tantrumed, the book argued, and the key to dealing with the problem was pretty much to love one's child in spite of it and just ride it out.

Charlotte had just had one of her out-of-the-blue fits about nothing, and I was trying, against my own inclination to haul out and damage her, not to do what the cursed book referred to as "having a tantrum back at my child." That is, I was sitting at the computer, actively doing nothing: not arguing with her, not threatening her, not responding at all, not making faces or throwing anything, and not even getting up out of my chair to follow her when she stomped into her own room and slammed the door.

The house was silent. I don't know where my husband and my other daughter were. Somehow when these fits came on Charlotte, they were directed at me and no one else, and whoever might have given me direction—Kris, Lulu, God—just seeped into the carpet and out of sight like spilled milk. I was alone.

So, there I sat. No longer playing Minesweeper on the computer, which is what I did in those days whenever I was stressed. Not planning any punishments or even an attempt to smooth things over and reconnect with Charlotte by lying that I was sorry for *her* tantrum. Not really thinking at all but just trying to escape the moment by willing myself out of it and into the silence. I don't know how long I sat there, maybe a minute, maybe ten, but suddenly Charlotte was with me in the silence. She appeared at my side without my having heard the click of her door or her typically heavy tread on the floor.

"I'm sorry," she told me, looking at the carpet, and she moved one of my arms aside so she could climb, in the horsey style she prefers, onto my lap. "I don't even know why I was mad," she told me, articulating precisely the dilemma of the spirited child and the argument of the book. And then she told me how whenever she had one of these fits, it scared her. She could never remember why she had gotten so mad at me, she said. But being mad got so big, all of a sudden, that she couldn't help it. It just spilled out of her.

Her words sounded so eerily straight from the book that I kind of wondered later if she might have been secretly reading it, but I wasn't thinking about that at the moment. I just held her, savoring her confession, thinking that I did indeed have the best child in the entire universe.

I also worried about the whole thing afterwards, of course. I mean, contrary to the book's reassurances about the normalcy of Charlotte's behavior, her tantrums seemed to me like demon possession or, worse, some sort of horrible manic depression that would only intensify as she turned into a teenager and eventually would render her anorexic or suicidal. But, so far, the book is right, and I am wrong, and Charlotte has passed through this stage into a congenial child who now knows what her limits are. She has taught herself to go to bed early when she's tired and run around in the fields around our house when she's excited, because she knows she'll fall apart if she doesn't. And I try to see my demands as a parent in terms of her limits as well, remembering, as it also says in Proverbs 18, that a girl's spirit sustains her in sickness, but a crushed spirit who can bear? Even that hard-nosed, do-the-right-thing Paul, who almost certainly never had kids unless he did so out of wedlock, urges us not to embitter or even exasperate our children (Colossians 3:21 and Ephesians 6:4) but to stave off their discouragement.

I suspect you're wondering, *What does any of this have to do with my struggle with remorse?* I was, too, until I thought back to the beginning and realized what I am about to tell you, here, in this book, for all the world to read if they care to: I am ashamed.

I am ashamed that I am not a naturally more loving person, that I had to read some cock-eyed book to learn that the most important thing in parenting is to love my own child. I am ashamed that I always believe I'm right and everyone else is wrong. I am ashamed that I hate the truth-tellers I encounter—like the apostle Paul, for example—because they show me up. I am ashamed that, a few weeks ago, I hated one of my most respected colleagues and friends, the one who gave the sermon on the prodigal son, for beginning a response to my public expression of justified outrage with, "Well, the gracious thing to do is . . ." I am ashamed that I never really pray for anyone but myself, certainly not for my enemies or even for those I am temporarily mad at. I am ashamed, even, of the impulse to go back into this paragraph and, wherever I admit shame, soften my offense—by saying I *almost* never pray for others, for example, and *hardly ever* for my enemies—or to add the phrase "like many others" or "like many of you" to soften shame's blow to my own pride by making someone else share it.

I am recording my shame here because it will leave me, momentarily and probably permanently. And the good news from the pigpen is, God doesn't care. He's bought me a ring and a robe already, a sweet chariot and a mansion, and he just doesn't give a rip that I don't deserve it.

Relevant and cited scriptural passages: Proverbs 13:24 and 18:14, Matthew 26:47–56 and 27:1–10, Mark 14:43–47, Luke 15 and 22:47–50, John 18:3–11, Colossians 3:21, and Ephesians 6:4.

Other references:

Don Balla. Chapel presentation. John Brown University. 9 April 2002.

Mary Sheedy Kurcinka. *Raising Your Spirited Child: A Guide for Parents Whose Child Is More Intense, Sensitive, Perceptive, Persistent, Energetic.* New York: HarperCollins, 1991.

John Newton. "Amazing Grace." Circa. 1772.

William Shakespeare. *Richard II.* 1597.

15

Intercessory Prayer

I've never been very happy with my prayers for others. First of all, I don't pray enough of them. I consciously hold myself back from saying, as many of my Christian friends do when someone talks about some problem, "Well, I'll be praying for you." I say that only in extreme cases of not knowing anything else to say, and usually, even then, I try to limit my personal involvement in the promise. When someone's parent I never met or even heard a story about dies and the conversation about it is going on too long and I absolutely can't think how to end it, I might say, "Well, my family will be praying for you," an expression of commiseration that provides a desirable sense of finality and an opportunity for me to leave without committing myself personally to prayer.

Not, mind you, that I think there's anything wrong with promising to pray for others. It's just that, in my case, the promise is likely to be a lie. I either forget to pray, or forget to tell my family to pray, or didn't really take the person's suffering, not being my own, seriously to being with. More often than not, I don't really mean it when I say it, and, even when I do, my prayers for others are always less important to me than my prayers for myself.

Now I'm sure you're not wanting to hear any more from me, because I have revealed myself to be a self-centered ass, who lies about the most holy of our Christian undertakings and uses foul language like *ass* to boot, but I have to go a few steps further into this confession before I can reveal myself to be the nice, loveable writer I usually am. Here we go.

Even when I do mean what I say, when I do feel consumingly bad for another person and take pains to remember the person in my own infrequent prayers, it seems to me I can't do it. I start out praying for the person, and I end up praying for myself. *Oh Lord, help my friend or my sister or my student,* I start out, and before long I'm asking him to help *me* solve whatever problems this person's problem is causing *me. Help* me *figure out how to deal with this student's anger, or my sister's bitter depression,* I pray.

I even have this problem when I'm praying for my own off-spring, the two little girls who used to be inside of me, who—as they once described the experience when they were even younger—drank my blood to stay alive. I mean, these two are my own flesh. You would think, if I could genuinely eliminate my own desires from a prayer for anyone else, it would be for these girls. But no. Some time ago, my husband was vacuuming and came across a prayer Charlotte had written out and hidden underneath some wadded up clothes that, from the smell of them, should have been put in the hamper weeks earlier. Charlotte was in the third grade at the time. My husband made me sit down at the kitchen table to read it. "Dear God and Jesus," she began. I can't tell you how it thrilled me to read these words. I read on:

Justin asked me out about 5 months ago. I was having fun going out with him. We kissed a few times (on the cheek). But the last few days he has been flirting with Karin (who already has a boyfriend) alot. I either want him to act like a boyfriend or I want to break up! I don't know how to tell him that. please help me.

♀ Charlotte

Now you need to understand that I am one of these tight-minded parents who does not want her children to repeat her own mistakes. I have read Neil Postman's wise book, *The Disappearance of Childhood,* and I have taken pains to avoid the early sexualization of my children and the evil influences of the media, which we limit considerably in our household by having a television but no cable or satellite and not even an antenna big enough to pick up more than one network station out of Fort Smith, Arkansas, and some grainy PBS shows. My daughters and I have talked about marital sex and being in love and recently, in response to Charlotte's alarming question in the car about how someone could bring herself to kill her own baby by having an abortion, the problem of losing one's head when in love and not thinking about the possible consequences of sex in the passion of the moment.

In the spirit of Ecclesiastes, I have set time limits for the girls, designed to celebrate their entry into various thresholds of maturity. At thirteen, the beginning of their teenage years, they may pierce their ears. At sixteen, they may call a boy their boyfriend and invite him over or go places with him with adults in attendance. At eighteen, they may be alone with a boy on an official date. Never at any age and under any circumstances should they drive drunk or let someone drive them who is. And so on.

And here I find Charlotte, the elder and more obedient and

attentive to my rules of my two daughters, not only "going out" with and kissing a boy half her size—a boy who won't eat anything but pizza and who had the audacity to call up the other day for my advice about a present he wanted to get her ("What does Charlotte like better? Giraffes or zebras?")—but DOING IT ON THE SLY, in conscious and intentional and concealed disobedience of my loving mandates.

And what was my prayer for her, you wonder? Keep my daughter safe from harm? Help her learn what she needs to learn here? Grow her into a strong, faith-filled wife and mother? No. *Help* me *to know what to do*, I prayed. *Help* me *to make her be the kind of person I want her to be. Help* me. *Solve this problem for* me. *Console* me.

A friend of mine once told me she has prayed for her son's future wife ever since he was a baby. I've tried to do the same for my daughters' future husbands, but I can't. I can't imagine what kind of men my daughters might marry, if they marry at all. Or anyway, it upsets me when I do try to imagine. How can I pray for men like that?

Sometimes I genuinely desire to pray for people, usually people with quite sensational problems that I happen to hear about—like an uncontrollable urge to view internet pornography all the time or some horrific illness—or else unsaved people like me before I was a Christian. Old friends. Members of my family. People who hate Christians or, worse, mistakenly think they *are* Christians not because they believe themselves forgiven through the death and resurrection of the Son of Man but because they belong to a club they call church that burdens them with all sorts of membership requirements. They attend with a certain regularity and don't commit whatever happen to be that church's favorite sins or at least successfully pretend not to; therefore, they think they are home free.

My childhood friend Melanie has always suffered from allergies. As a child, she could never spend much time with the animals her family had—goats, chickens, sheep, calves, a lame horse—without getting red and swollen and itchy around her mouth and eyes. Melanie truly loved animals, too. Unlike me, she didn't mind their smells or demands. She fed and played with them. She bolted around the immense field that was her family's yard with these big rambunctious dogs they had. The dogs would get so excited they'd bark themselves hoarse and even knock her over sometimes, but she'd get up laughing and hug them and romp some more. I was always afraid of big dogs and, when I was over at Melanie's house, watched from somewhere close to the house so I could get back inside quickly if I had to. When Melanie came back from playing with the dogs, her face would be red and puffy, and she had to use this thick cream that never really soaked in to keep from scratching herself raw.

My parents regarded allergies with cynicism. Coming home and saying someone you knew had allergies was tantamount to saying the person was prissy or a show-off or, worst of all, a hypochondriac. Somehow, although I have had allergic reactions myself, and both my children are prone to allergies, I seem to have inherited their skepticism. A couple of my elderly relatives have a long list of foods they can't eat. Eggs. Onions. Chocolate. Garlic. Soybean products in anything except the processed foods they live on. Spices of any kind except for the spices in the Cajun food they loved back when they lived in Louisiana. It's true they are sickly—as anyone would be who lived almost exclusively on undercooked bacon, sweets of any kind, and Swann's frozen hotdogs and fish sticks. Once, though, I mentioned their allergies disparagingly to Melanie, and she defended them angrily. I still feel ashamed about it.

A few years ago, I went to Colorado to see Melanie, who was visiting there from Germany for a family reunion, and I hardly recognized her when I went to pick her up at the airport. In fact, I recognized her beautiful little seven-year-old daughter Rebecca first, even though I hadn't seen her since she was a toddler. She lay asleep on an airport bench near the baggage claim. She looked just as Melanie had as a child, with the same long, full, caramel-colored hair I had always envied, the same delicate features and pale skin. I couldn't see Mel anywhere in the crowd of people near her. Then I heard my name. It was ninety-some degrees out, but Melanie wore long sleeves and a scarf around her neck. Her face and hands and what I could see of her red wrists were thickly coated with cream. Her allergies had gotten so out of control in the past years since I had seen her that she had recently had to spend six weeks in a special hospital for skin illnesses far from the Bavarian town where they live.

She told me the details with great reluctance. So many remedies tried and failed. Finally going to homeopaths. The skin hospital had been her last resort. For the first weeks of her stay, the nurses wrapped her entire body in wet rags, she said, using slightly wrong and in this case alarming vocabulary, *rags* for *cloths*, the way longtime expatriates often do. Then various experimental regimens—herbal waters, creams, dietary changes. Six weeks long. The itching. Not getting to see her husband or Rebecca but once, briefly, in all that time. Alone. I couldn't imagine the torture of what must have been her life during those weeks.

When I left Colorado, I didn't tell Melanie I'd pray for her, although I intended to do so. I didn't know what her views were on faith, and I didn't want to risk offending her. I remembered how I felt about others' prayers back before I became a Christian.

When my Christian friends promised to pray for me, as they often did, I worried that they would pray my future as *they*, not *I*, would have it. Or that several of them might pray at cross-purposes to one another and God, if he actually did exist, would get mixed up.

When Melanie and I were children, faith had never been a barrier between us: I was Catholic, and she was Quaker, the faiths of our parents. I attended Melanie's church and youth group activities from time to time, and I loved everything I learned about Quakers. Since our childhoods, though, my mom had died after long years of suffering, and Melanie had lost her father and brother. Both of our childhood faiths had staggered and evolved—hers to what I guessed was the taciturn agnosticism of many of my old friends and mine to unwilling atheism and, only much later, born-again Christianity.

How did Jesus pray for the suffering and the sick, back in the days when they, like Melanie with her allergies, had little hope of a cure beyond a miracle? I'm sure I don't know. Every time I thought of Melanie, I felt bad for her. And I thought of her often, but my prayers felt empty, as if I had no confidence in the miracles that were needed here, as if, despite my faith in a healing God, I knew no cleverer hope than new doctors and herbal remedies and wet rags.

The other day my division chair, a jolly and devout Episcopalian, sent the women of our division an e-mail of some fill-in-the-blank prayers she found helpful. She didn't know about my long term struggle with intercessory prayer, I hope, or that it had been getting worse recently—that I've come to this ugly, loveless place where I'm convinced I'm simply incapable of caring about anyone's troubles but my own, that I'm just one hundred percent selfish and that's that and there's nothing I can do about it, and it's a good thing Jesus died for the truly lost and loveless because that's the only way I'm going to get anywhere but in a hole in the ground and then hell.

The e-mail included intercessory prayers for one's spouse, family members who were ill, anyone else who was ill or had a special problem, and a Christian friend's spiritual growth. The prayers were beautiful, much more so than my own efforts, invoking God as the only "source of health and healing," of strength, forgiveness, love. In five prayers, each a paragraph long, the word *help* is used only five times, once in the prayer for the spouse—"Help us to forgive one another's failings and grant us patience, kindness, cheerfulness and the spirit of placing the well-being of one another ahead of self"—and the other four times for the family member who is ill. In my much more perfunctory prayers, I say the word *help* much more often. Sometimes it's all I can say.

I need to pray for my spouse, I know, but here again I find my prayers irritatingly self-centered. *Help him to quit doing what I hate. Help him realize how wrong he is, and how right I am. Help him to understand me and do what I want*, I pray, but not, *Help me to understand him and do what he wants.* Wouldn't that be an amazing prayer? I can't pray it. Instead I pray things like, *Heavenly Father, please make Kris stop being so sensitive and taking everything I say so personally.* And never, *Heavenly Father, make me a kinder, gentler person. Keep me from attacking and criticizing the ones I love. Let every word that leaves my mouth say what I mean, and let what I mean be selfless. Let me not be me at all, Lord, but rather the me you see through the sin-obscuring blood of your sacrificed son.*

Sometimes, I worry about my inability to pray for others—and all of my other failures as a Christian. Although I steadfastly avoid the book of James and devour those passages in John and Paul and elsewhere that assure me that nothing I do or don't do can damage my salvation, which derives from faith alone, nevertheless I sometimes secretly doubt my promised transformation into the image of Christ. Will I be one of those Jesus mentions, who cry, "Lord, Lord!" but never really do what he says and are tossed out of heaven on the very brink of entry?

Other times my faith is stronger, and I imagine God's vision of me as a sort of a reverse MRI that scans the whole body searching not for sickness but some lurking wellness—not for what I look like on the outside but for the goodness beneath all the sin, for who, in Christ, I really am.

My Calvinist friends say there's no goodness in us at all, and this makes me feel bleak. No wonder I can't get out of myself to pray for others. There's no me in there to get out!

In the small Oklahoma town where I live, certain people are commonly referred to as prayer warriors. Usually they're old people, often unmarried. People known to keep and update long lists of who all is sick and needs prayed for. They pray for the church, for individual members of the body who are sick or struggling, for the wayward youth, for our leaders, for their nieces and nephews, for those more aged and infirm than they, for people in the local newspaper or on the staticky radio station that covers the latest hospital admittances and releases, for anyone in need they hear about, for me, probably, without my knowing it. When there is news of some more exciting trouble than usual, someone organizes a prayer chain, and the warriors are always front and center and pulling up the rear. When warriors die, their prayers are their legacy, totted up and lauded like the Purple Hearts and grandchildren in the eulogies of others. Prayer warriors, even while still alive, are routinely referred to as men and women of God.

I would like to be one of them. I'd like to be called that. More than that, though, I'd like to pray my daughter's prayer on her behalf and mean it. *Help her learn about men, how to talk to them, how much to ask, how much to give, how to seek you in them. Help her.*

I'd like to pray Melanie's prayer—straight out of what I can only imagine to be her hurts and angers and fears. I want to pray, *Hey, you there, you powerful Creator who made my father and my shiny brother and then let them die. You loving ruler who allowed the Holocaust, of which my mother, one of your so-called chosen people, was a victim. You there, you God you, can you eradicate this allergy? Can you turn six weeks of being wrapped like a mummy into something besides wasted time, time away from my husband and little daughter, time I don't even tell my friends about for fear of boring or worrying them with my troubles?*

But even if I could pray such a prayer and mean it, my words would only be guesses, prayed from far away, from outside my friend's experience, from the safe place of my own stunted love for others, my own secret unbeliefs.

In case any of you, my readers, share my problems as a pray-er, I have made up my own fill-in-the-blank prayer for all occasions. It's all about me, of course, but as that's all I can do, it'll have to suffice:

Spirit of God, who hears my groans and speaks their true meaning to the Father, hear my prayer. Let my desire to pray for _____ be my prayer on his/her behalf. Take the *me* out of my prayer and fill it in with the selfless love of the Son. Hear not only my groans, Holy Spirit, but my fleeting compassion, my infrequent notice of my neighbor. When, through the fog of my self-concern, I *notice* another's pain or need, another's struggle, translate that, too, like my groans, into a prayer of great worth. Or, better yet, groan for others on my behalf—for the ones I love and the ones whose care and nurture have been entrusted into my fumbling hands and atrophied heart. Groan for them, Companion of what soul I have, and hear their groans and prayers, however angry and rebellious, and pass them on, edited, to the Father.

And if God feels the power go out of him and asks who groaned—if, perchance, he happens to find out about my inadequacies as a pray-er—I hope the Holy Spirit will intervene for me and say, "Oh well, you know, she meant to pray. She said she would, after all. She would have prayed, you know, for this poor sufferer had she been that person herself. She had the best of intentions."

Relevant and cited scriptural passages: Ecclesiastes 3:1–8, Matthew 7:15–27, Luke 6:43–49, John 6:28–29, Romans 7 and 8, 2 Corinthians 3:18, and James.

Other references:

John Bunyan. *The Pilgrim's Progress from This World to That Which Is to Come.* 1678.

Neil Postman. *The Disappearance of Childhood.* New York: Delacorte, 1982.

"A Prayer for Healing" and "Spouse's Prayer." Catholic Doors Ministry. www.catholicdoors.com, 2001.

16

Rethinking Our Miracles: Some Thoughts on Doubt

In John Bunyan's *The Pilgrim's Progress from This World to That Which Is to Come*, when Christian and Hopeful finally arrive at the Celestial City, their fellow pilgrim, Ignorance, shows up there too, but without the requisite Roll of Election. The same Shining Ones who welcomed Christian and Hopeful in, now bind Ignorance hand and foot and throw him out, recalling those who Jesus tells us will cry "Lord, Lord" but not enter the kingdom of heaven. A seventeenth century contemporary of Bunyan, Calvinist theologian Robert Bolton, describes the same disturbing end of some who call themselves believers: "How many go to hell," he writes, "with a vaine hope of heaven; whose chiefest cause of damnation is their false persuasion, and groundlesse presumption of salvation."

From time to time since I became a Christian, having experienced a midlife conversion nothing short of a miracle, I have nevertheless worried about the sad fate of such seeming Christians. I have more than once imagined *myself* before the Father, expecting to be clasped in welcome only to find myself shunned and rejected after all. Nor can I easily accept the pat reassurances of those who preach that these "Lord, Lord" criers are shrewd hypocrites, who use false histrionics to try and sneak their way into heaven and don't really think they are Christians at all. They never truly desire God's company but merely its attendant pleasures and an escape from hell.

The apostles themselves, when Jesus told them one of their number would betray him, asked one after the next, "Is it I, Lord?" Apparently, even they, Jesus' most faithful followers, whom he hand selected one by one, struggled with doubt of their own faith on the eve of their Savior's death. Following the Reformation, apparently to address similar worries of their congregations, theologians wrote numerous books detailing how believers might determine if they were among the elect.

What are we to make of such fears, especially in light of equally mysterious promises—suggested by Paul's unsettling choice of words—as election and predestination? Is there really the possibility that, thinking ourselves among the saved, we will, like Bunyan's Ignorance, arrive at heaven's door without our Roll of Election? And, more importantly, is it okay—might it even profit us—to worry about this eventuality in advance?

When I first became a Christian, the leader of my Sunday school class startled me one day by announcing that she knew *she* was going to heaven. She sounded smug to me, like people who tell you they know what *they* would do if someone held them up at gunpoint or if *their* Jewish neighbors started being herded into trains and shipped off to work camps with long smokestacks.

I have since become accustomed to such confident statements of faith from my fellow Christians, though. My children, for example, say the same sort of thing from time to time, and I am glad of it, even though I know they do not understand many of the details of their faith. One day when they were small, we were driving down the road, and they told me they wished we could all be raptured then and there but were worried that the roof of the car would somehow impede their upward progress. Do other believers—those of cleaner, simpler faith, like my former Sunday school leader and my daughters—have no doubt? Is my own struggle a burden or a crutch in my pilgrimage?

It is the nature of the doubter, I think, to answer questions with questions. So, the only answers I have to my own questions are further questions, mysterious stairways I ascend and never reach the actual tops of but only landings from which to gaze back down over how far I have come. I offer a few of them here.

Mary, Jesus' mom, a virgin, was visited by an angel who told her she would be impregnated by God himself and bear God's son. And when this miracle indeed came to pass and the shepherds reported their own visit from angels concerning the birth, Mary, we're told, "treasured up all these things and pondered them in her heart"—along with, in all likelihood, other miracles she must have witnessed as Jesus was growing up, culminating in him changing water into wine at her request.

Years later, though, at the peak of Jesus' ministry, when crowds followed him wherever he went and teachers of the law were accusing him of being "the prince of demons," his family became alarmed and "went to take charge of him, for they said, 'He is out of his mind'" (Mark 3:21). Crazy. Insane. All those miracles they were hearing about merely the misbehaviors of someone mentally ill. We are not told explicitly who in Jesus' family doubted his sanity, but some verses later his mother and brothers show up looking for him at the house where he is preaching. It is easy enough to understand Jesus' brothers' doubt. After all, they were born after him, and what sibling has not scoffed at an older sibling's wild claims? It would take a lot of healings and resurrections for me to believe my big sister Sharon was God.

But what of Mary? Her faith in Jesus' divinity had to have been as unassailable as it gets. His miraculous birth was not only prophesied in advance but heralded by an angel and ultimately performed on her own body. Unrelated shepherds and wisemen confirmed her experiences with reports of similar miracles they had witnessed. She had heard, seen, felt the truth of Jesus' divinity claims and even tested them out with a miracle on demand. Could it actually be that, having experienced firsthand—having in fact *pondered, treasured*—the miracle of Jesus' divine birth, Mary herself thought her son's claims the ravings of a madman? Did even Mary doubt Jesus' divinity? Could even she—who responded to Gabriel's strange announcement with the words, "May it be to me as you have said"—could even Mary have succumbed to that most compelling of doubts, the doubt of the believing mother who fears for her children and would rescue them even from the hand of God to the safety of her own care?

And then there's Peter. Having just walked on water—and not just any water but wind-buffeted waves "a considerable distance from land" (Matthew 14:24)—having just felt that water as solid as an asphalt road beneath his feet, why did he suddenly lose faith in its solidity and sink?

Finally, Jesus himself, upon the cross, knowing with absolute certainty that his death would be temporary, that soon he would be reunited with his Father in heaven, cried out, "My God, my God! Why have you forsaken me?" Why did he feel abandoned, I've always wondered. Had he forgotten that this was part of the plan, that God loved him above all others, that his Father would never forsake him? How are *we* to believe the promise that we will survive death, if God's own Son evidently didn't?

My former Sunday school leader and several preachers have attempted to address my questions by explaining that God the Father *did*, in fact, abandon his son on the cross because, having taken upon himself the sins of the world, Jesus was repulsive to God and could not be in his presence. But I am not convinced. After all, Jesus, when it comes right down to it, *is* God. How can he actually forsake himself? And anyway, this mystery aside, why do his words sound so familiar, so like the unbelief of my own past, so exactly like my own internal voice that yet speaks these fears, the voice of my doubt?

Recently, I was talking to my daughter Charlotte about a miracle we both witnessed a couple of years ago. It was a minor miracle, nothing to get too excited about, but a miracle nonetheless. Our beagle, Layla Flower, had had puppies several weeks earlier. I had awakened the girls in the night to see the births, and they had watched the puppies emerge. In the days that followed they watched the pups nurse and grow and open their eyes and start to walk around in the mudroom.

Eventually, the puppies got too loud and messy to keep in the house, so we moved them to our old dairy barn across the road, where they could roam around and bark and chew things in all contentedness until they were old enough to sell. My husband Kris fed and watered the puppies and their mother there, and one evening he came back to the house with the grim news that the girls' favorite puppy, Midnight, the only black one and the only one they had named, had gotten caught in the swinging door to the feed room and broken her leg. Kris said there was probably nothing we could do for so small a puppy that we weren't planning to keep anyway, but the girls were so distraught that he let me call the vet and told us to get a box ready to put the puppy in for the trip. Then he went back to the barn to fetch Midnight.

The girls were crying, so I suggested we pray while we waited, and the girls dutifully asked God to heal Midnight, and I silently added a plea that it wouldn't cost a fortune if he did. Just calling the vet into the office for an after hours emergency call, I knew, would add fifty dollars to his fee. When Kris got back, we all cried some more over the little puppy, which lay eyes closed and silent in the shoebox, her broken leg bent unnaturally forward. One of the girls touched a finger to the hurt place, and Midnight yelped weakly but did not open her eyes.

Half an hour later, Dr. McCarver gingerly gathered the puppy up from the shoebox, felt along her leg, then stood her up on the metal examining table and pronounced her entirely unharmed. As if to prove this true, Midnight barked enthusiastically and skittered across the table, and the girls shrieked, "Answered prayer! Answered prayer!" Dr. McCarver sent us away, refusing payment for his services because, as he said, he hadn't done anything.

That was our miracle, a small but powerful one for my daughters and me. And, even though Midnight escaped when we put the puppies outside in a pen a few weeks later and disappeared forever, her recovery from the broken leg deepened my faith as significantly as a glass of water changed to wine before my greedy lips. However, when Charlotte mentioned Midnight recently, she couldn't even remember the miracle.

"But Midnight's leg wasn't really broken," she insisted. "We just *thought* it was!"

"No, Daddy heard it crack, and we saw it all bent and touched it and prayed about it. Don't you remember?" I urged. "Don't you remember telling Dr. McCarver that it was answered prayer?"

But she continued to argue that God hadn't *really* answered our prayer to heal Midnight's broken leg but had merely let us be mistaken about its brokenness in the first place.

In this logical rejection of the faith she once had, I see myself at an earlier time. I was impressed by the stories of steadfast faith of my Catholic upbringing. The centurion whose faith was so great that he didn't even need to witness the healing of his servant to believe it could and would be done. The dramatically unshakable faith of the early church martyrs in my *Little Pictorial Lives of Saints.*

As I mentioned earlier, my favorite saint was Polycarp, an elderly bishop of Smyrna, who, under persecution, pragmatically stated that it was hardly worth his while to renounce his faith since he was old and had spent his life believing and was so near to his prize. As a child, I thought I shared this faith, but when troubles engulfed my family when I was a teenager, I dismissed whatever miniscule faith I had then, not to mention the more extreme examples of it I had admired in others. God had plainly forsaken me and my family.

And when my mother, who had been a lukewarm Catholic at best, suddenly took to caressing a Bible she had never read and couldn't read now and saying over and over again, "Jesus loves me, Jesus loves me," God's forsaking and her poor benighted ignorance of it were all the more convincing to me. It never even occurred to me during those years that God might have a plan for my mother or that he could actually heal her, that he could work his miracles without me believing in them or even crediting them to him at all. But evidently he did have a plan. Much later, years after her death, I finally realized that my mother, though then blind and so severely memory impaired as to be incapable of recognizing her own children, had nevertheless met and fallen in love with the son of God, a miracle that first increased my unbelief then caused my faith to flourish.

Can faith admit doubt? Can doubt actually *grow* faith? Peter, the Rock on whom Jesus built his church; Mary, whose future livelihood Jesus attended to even as he was dying on the cross; and Jesus' own amazing resurrection all promise that it can—that, despite my worries and many questions, I will never cry "Lord, Lord" in vain.

Relevant and cited scriptural passages: Matthew 7:21–23, 8:5–13, 14:22–36, 26:22, and 27:45–47; Mark 3:20–34, 14:19, 15:33–35, and 3:20–35; Luke 2:18–20 and 2:51; John 2:1–11 and 19:25–27; Romans 8:29–30 and 9:6–13; and Ephesians 11:4–6.

Other references:

Robert Bolton. *The Four Laste Things: Death, Judgment, Hell, and Heaven.* London: G. Miller, 1635. (p.26)

John Bunyan. *The Pilgrim's Progress from This World to That Which Is to Come.* 1678.

Christopher Love. *A Treatise on Effectual Calling and Election.* 1658.

Thomas Manton. *A Treatise of Self-Denial.* 1689.

John Gilmary Shea. *Little Pictorial Lives of Saints.* 1878.

17

Joseph's Dreams

If we read the narrative of Jesus' birth from the perspective of Joseph, his earthly father, it is hardly a story of unmitigated joy. If it were fiction, though—as some Bible scholars claim it is, constructed after the fact for theological purposes—it would probably be a rather funny story, in a grim sort of way.

Imagine: You're in love with the sweetest, nicest, best looking, and certainly the most morally upright of all the girls in Nazareth, and even both your sets of parents agree that you two were meant for each other. So, you get betrothed, and everything is going fine. You've got a steady job, and she's eager to start a family, and you're just about to get married when she turns up pregnant by somebody else.

"It's okay," she reassures you, as if bad weren't bad enough. "I haven't been sleeping around. Honest. I mean, an angel came and visited me and told me God himself is the father. I'm serious. I didn't do anything wrong. He overshadowed me. I don't even remember it. If the angel hadn't told me it had happened, I wouldn't even know."

She tells you the baby's name, Jesus, a name that never was in your family or hers, probably the new boyfriend's dad or something. And worst of all, instead of being shamefaced or even glum about any of this, she's positively ecstatic. She even makes up a song about how wonderful God is and how his son will be a king, who will bring down the high up and raise up the low down, that he will be, in short, the savior we've all been waiting for.

Fine thoughts, you're thinking. God has made her pregnant. Yeah, right. And she looks for all the world like she's telling the truth when she sings this, but when you tell your two best buddies, they're making all these jokes about her chastity and your stupidity.

So, not only is your girlfriend pregnant by someone else, but she's obviously deranged, because how else could she say such things and act like she's telling the God's truth? But you don't really have the heart to make a big deal about it. You've heard of women being stoned to death for less. A messy way to die that would surely reflect badly on you. And anyway, you think, that would be punishing her for being crazy, and because you still love her and, even though you feel betrayed, you can't bring yourself to believe she's lying.

So, you start looking around for a lawyer or a rabbi or someone who can undo the betrothal papers without a big to-do so that you two can go your own ways. It takes a few days to figure out how the thing is done. They never taught you anything in your Bible study class about how to get unbetrothed. You don't even know what to call it.

Meanwhile, Mary goes off to visit her cousin Elizabeth, an old lady who also just came up pregnant and is making all sorts of strange claims about *her* baby. It seems this brand of craziness runs in Mary's family. The cousin's husband, a really good guy in everyone's opinion, is so embarrassed about the whole thing with Elizabeth getting pregnant and saying such things that he hasn't said a word since the day he found out. And you're like, this is too weird.

So, anyway, you just about have an arrangement lined up with this guy that makes his living divorcing people. He doesn't have a word for undoing a betrothal either, but he says it can be done. Then Mary comes back from her cousin's and you tell her how it's going to be, and she seems sad, but grateful not to have to be stoned. But you haven't quite gotten up the guts to perform the total emotional suicide of telling your parents.

Mom has already ordered the wedding announcements and so forth. She invites you to supper, a prenuptial celebration such as she's been putting on every weekend since the betrothal. You plan it out: tonight I will tell them. You rehearse it. At dinner, you drink more wine than usual, getting ready, and at one point you're just about to say, "Listen up! I have something to tell you." But at that precise moment, someone raises the inevitable toast—mazel tov!—and your courage fails you. The words froth up, like some foul burp, and you end up going to bed having said nothing.

That night you dream, of course, about Mary and angels and God fathering human babies. You dream that you are naming the baby, that God has told you to name the baby Jesus, and you are raising him up like a glass of wine, someone else's son—mazel tov!—and announcing his name to your assembled family. Someone is singing crazily, and this big brawny angel with hairy arms is lifting his glass, too, saying something about the baby saving people from their sins and fulfilling various prophecies. Mazel tov.

Or perhaps it wasn't that way at all. Most of the details are missing, unfortunately, and we're left to surmise, as we usually are with ancient texts, especially biblical ones, much of what actually went on. Or perhaps, as those Bible scholars argue, the whole story is made up to house the prophecies that the tax collector Matthew wanted to get across to his audience. Well, here's what we know from the text: Mary was pregnant and must have told Joseph something about it that made him want to divorce her quietly. Then he had a dream in which an angel reassured him that everything Mary must have said was true.

The part I struggle with is that dream. Or, rather, that Joseph believes his dreams to be messages from God. There end up being four more of these dreams that all come at crucial decision-making moments in his struggle to be God's earthly father, and I always wonder, were his dreams different from other people's dreams? Or could it be that *all* dreams are God talking to us, after a fashion, if we just had Joseph's faith?

I have dreams every night in which all sorts of people do and say all sorts of weird things, and I never regard them as direct communications from God. Once, I even had what I now regard as a prophetic dream, given that the event it seemed to be about really did come to pass at about the same time the dream occurred. But I've always explained the dream away as, at best, a paranormal glitch of sorts, a bulging of the supernatural realm into the natural one we live in or, at worst, an intriguing coincidence.

The regular dreams I have, though, seem to share a certain chaotic resistance to clean explication. How could God be talking to me if the message is so messy? How did Joseph unravel his dreams such that he knew what to do?

Just about every morning I take one or two of my dreams down to the breakfast table for my husband to interpret. It seems to me each new dream has exactly the same basic elements as the ones the day before. Their main characters are almost always changelings, starting out as one of my family members from the past, my mom or dad or one of my siblings, and then metamorphosing into my husband or one of my students or a merging of both of my daughters into a son I never had. There are always urgent ideas, strong emotions such as fear or frustration or pleasure, and remembered events or fragments of speech recognizable from a day or two before. Typically, patterns of problems repeat and occasionally resolve themselves: the apparent storyline of one part of the dream is told again with different characters or a slightly different outcome, as if to say, "Here, try this out." Or, "How 'bout this?"

My dreams are, in brief, rather like the visions of Revelation: full of emergencies and repetitions and weird composite creatures. In both my dreams and John's visions, otherwise inauspicious objects or themes recur in episode after episode and acquire symbolic relevance. A house, my teeth, animals, making a phone call, bowls, lamps, deserts, remembered places where I've never been. Most dream interpreters these days, like Freud and Daniel and the Old Testament Joseph before them, appear to think that my dream symbols mean the same thing as everyone else's, that there is a collective dream vocabulary—teeth are your sense of self worth, branches or baskets are days, men on horses one's impending death—translations as blithe and useless as hieroglyphics to the modern dreamer.

At the breakfast table, my husband, with that frightening efficiency of the innocent, cuts right through it all—symbols, characters, emotions—to find direct representations of what he thinks are the things currently bothering me in my life. His interpretations are often instructive but usually reveal more about what's bothering *him* than about my dream might actually mean. Our conversation goes something like this:

"Babe, I had this dream in which my sister Sharon brings this cat to our house, only it isn't really our house now but a house in Pompeii where, in my dream, we had been living for a while. In my dream you are a farmer again, and I am always making bread. But anyway, you bring in this cat you found on the road—because my sister changes into you—and it has all these gashes in it that you want me to sew up. So, after I spend a long time not finding first a needle and then thread, I eventually manage to start sewing, but the cat turns out to be dead. Actually, I know that it never had been alive to begin with, but nothing I can say will make you believe it. You are my sister again, and you keep saying, 'No, it's alive. You're just saying that.'"

Kris is making the coffee and, it seems to me, ignoring what I'm saying the whole time, and I'm just about to say so when he says, "Your sister is my mom, and you think she shouldn't drive the girls to Siloam this Sunday when we're in Tulsa."

"But what does that have to do with my dream?" I whine. And he explains: the cat is the children, dead or about to be dead, and the Sharon-person who changes into him is his mom. And what he tells me has nothing to do with my dream, but he is so certain of his interpretation that I know he's really worried about the kids being driven by his mom. So, after we're finished talking, I call up Mamaw and tell her we don't want the girls to go to Siloam with her to her sister's house after all, and can't Uncle Dean and Aunt Lorraine just drive here and eat at her house?

Here's the thing. Joseph went at his dreams in a totally different way. He had to have; otherwise, he would never have been so certain about what they meant. He went to bed worried—about marrying a pregnant woman, about taking care of a baby the king was trying to kill, about whether he should stay in Egypt or go back home, about where home was now that he'd been away for so long—and he woke up with a purpose and the certainty that his purpose was divinely inspired.

I'm thinking Joseph had no special gift of interpretation but merely an analytical method a lot more intentionally faithful than mine. He didn't ask Mary at the breakfast table or consult a dream dictionary. Instead, he stared right though the reassembled chaos of his dream to his hopes, buried there: that his wife-to-be was speaking the truth, that there would indeed be a Messiah, that God would protect him, that he had a true home, that his descendants would take possession of his enemies' cities, and that the boy he would raise as his son, God's son, would be blessed by all the nations of the earth. He chose to see hope in his dreams, instead of his fears, and to believe his hope to be true. Isn't that what the writer of Hebrews tells us that faith *is*, "being sure of what we hope for"—so sure that we can go forth without fear— "and certain of what we do not see"—even God's invisible qualities, which tend to get hidden under the mess?

How did Joseph understand that God had spoken to him? He sifted through his worries to find confirmation of that most essential promise: the promise that, incomprehensibly, he mattered to God and would have a role in displaying God's glory. Joseph peered into his dreams for the message that he—a nobody, a carpenter from the podunk town of Nazareth—was called to be the lover of God's own choice in a woman and the protector of his infant son. He accepted his dreams, like everything else in his life, as evidence that there was a hope worth waiting for, a future worth buying into, a love worth risking one's life and very sanity to believe in.

Don't misunderstand me. If anyone needed a visit from an angel, it seems to me, it was Joseph. And I know I've wished for as much myself to solve the petty miseries of my own life. What Joseph's story tells us, though, is that we matter to God. We are visited by angels nightly, but, unlike Joseph, we ignore them.

We matter to God. Inexplicably. Undeservedly. Even we dedicated Christians tend to forget this truth—or doubt it or altogether reject it—when we encounter trouble. It is difficult to understand why we matter, but we do. God is watching, listening to us, speaking promises into the cacophony of our worries and the certainty of their fulfillment into our most deeply buried hopes. To have faith, as Joseph did, all we have to do is pay attention as hope refracts what we see to reveal the future God has planned for his children. Faith means literally believing that in all things, even the crappiest ones, God works for the good of those who love him.

Relevant and cited scriptural passages: Genesis 37:5–11 and 40, Daniel 2 and 4, Matthew 1:18–25, Luke 1:26–56, Romans 8:28, Hebrews 11:1, and Revelation.

18

The Book and the Cup

In the damp basement it is raining, and the rain is raining into the existing dampness from some unknown source. Is there a broken window? An open door? A breach in the retaining wall? My daughters and I skirt the edges in search of a place to stand where it's not dripping. And all the while I hear voices from other unseen regions of the vast, black, wet space. Commiserating. Reassuring. Giving me various directions and invitations, but I can't see to follow them.

The voices sound foreign but are familiar to me. My daughters huddle together, away from me, and I want to hold the youngest, lift her and feel her stout legs around my middle, but she asks in her small voice, without approaching, if she and Charlotte can go outside and play.

In the rain? I'm thinking. I do not know if I am outraged or lamenting—both probably—and then Charlotte's real voice cries out from the next room, interrupting my dream, to tell me, angrily, that she's lost the socks she's been wearing on her hands for eleven days now to keep from sucking her thumb in her sleep.

"They're not in the bed," she tells me angrily, as I grope through the covers. "I've already looked," she says again, holding my arm impatiently.

Now both children are sitting up in the covers. It's early early morning, still dark, but near my time for getting up anyway, so I speak patiently, hoping to calm them back into their last, precious forty-five minutes of sleep. I want to drink my coffee, read, think about the day, in silence. I find the socks, in the bed, without comment, and the girls sink back.

Kris is still in the bathroom when I go downstairs, so I heat my own milk for coffee and froth it, then sit down to finish the puzzle the girls and I started days ago that's still spread out at my place on the table. It is a meadow scene with mountains in the distance. If I finish it, they have informed me, they will take it apart again so we can do it all together. I understood this at the time as a threat and haven't touched the puzzle, but I finish it now anyway to make space for my Bible and the cup. I am amazed to discover that we have not lost a single piece. The meadow is full of blurred flowers, and the distant mountains are a fake-looking photographic blue.

I resume thinking about yesterday's riddle: *From the days of John the Baptist until now, the kingdom of heaven has been forcefully advancing, and forceful men lay hold of it* (Matthew 11:12). I think about John in prison, soon to be beheaded, wanting to know if Jesus really is the Messiah, doubting the very essence of a faith for which he is willing to give up his life. In the King James Version my husband quotes from his own lifetime of wondering, it seems to mean the opposite: *And from the days of John the Baptist until now the kingdom of heaven suffereth violence, and the violent take it by force.* Both translations seem to hold the answer. They are equally beautiful, equally ambiguous. The New International

Version note explains that the Greek verb for "forcefully advancing" may be in either active or passive voice, making both readings semantically plausible. What does the passage mean?

Now it is years later. If it were not recorded, the dripping water dream would not even be a memory. Charlotte has long since quit sucking her thumb. The girls sleep in separate beds and wake me up at night only rarely, which is a blessing I have neglected, until now, to appreciate. There are more blessings I routinely forget: I no longer seek refuge in leaky shelters of uncertainty. And I am not in prison about to be beheaded. Also, it is not expected of me to know everything. In fact, in response to John the Baptist's doubting query if his cousin really *is* the promised savior, Jesus, amazingly, praises John, proclaiming that "Among those born of women there has not risen anyone greater than John the Baptist." He then goes on to include the rest of us doubters in his approval: "yet he who is least in the kingdom of heaven is greater than he" (Matthew 11:11).

I still don't have the faintest idea what it means that the kingdom of heaven is forcefully advancing or suffering violence or that forceful or violent men are laying hold of it or carrying it off. But for the moment this too is a blessing, a love message from God himself, to John and to me, that it is all right to doubt—that to doubt is to seek, and to seek is to hope, and to hope urgently, insistently, with certainty, is to have all the faith we need in order to survive whatever lies ahead.

Relevant and cited scriptural passages: Matthew 11:1–19 and Hebrews 11:1.

Progress

19

Blind Driver

Having grown up in Southern California, I have been to Disneyland many times. My family went at least once a year and whenever we had out-of-town guests. Back in those days, the entrance fee was nominal, and you bought books of tickets lettered A through E for the various rides. We stored the partially used up books of tickets in a kitchen drawer along with the address book and my mom's coupons. The tickets left were mostly A and B tickets for the kiddy rides, and when I was in high school, my friends and I would take those tickets and spend an evening riding Dumbos or spinning ourselves sick in the Flying Teacups.

Even after I grew up and left home and returned to Southern California only once a year to see my family—dutifully, almost reluctantly, and usually with some boyfriend in tow—we always visited Disneyland. Not out of any lingering excitement for my favorite rides or even the newer, scarier rides. Not to savor, as I did in childhood, a gigantic spiral lollipop or one of Disneyland's newer culinary treats, like their wonderful greasy churros, gritty with cinnamon sugar. Not even to show off the disarming pleasure

145

of the place to the boyfriend, who was invariably some foreign intellectual cynical about American theme parks in general and Disneyland in particular.

No, I returned for something more visceral, I think. The familiar terror of negotiating the older Santa Ana Freeway in one of my parents' boat-like cars. The smell of stagnant water and restaurant food in the dark wet womb of the Pirates of the Caribbean. The utter artificialness of everything at Disneyland, even the living trees, many of which are clipped into looming zoo animals or characters from the Disney movies. Disneyland is, in some sense, my notion of home: a self-satisfied conflation of the familiar with the absurd, of tawdry invention and homely joys, of treasures that do not last and yet seem to never fade away or die entirely.

On one such trip to Disneyland in my boyfriend years, we went with my older sister Sharon and her husband. Sharon and Tom were newlyweds and born-again Christians. Sharon was so newly born again she was like an actual newborn, relentlessly vocal about her faith but surprisingly friable, too. The unlikeliest topic might cause a theological outburst, and, like a mother with her baby, I tried to stave off embarrassment by avoiding anything I thought remotely likely to trigger a religious debate.

We strolled up Main Street to Disneyland proper, stopping in all the shops along the way. In my youth we never lingered in the shops but shot straight to our favorite rides, but now I was an adult, sight-seeing. We watched a woman torch a tube of glass into the shape of a hummingbird, then wandered through a candy shop, then stood with a small crowd and listened to a Dixieland band in red, white, and blue striped trousers play a staid ragtime piece. At each stop I was conscious of the boyfriend at my side, silently judging this kitsch, that hedonism, and that, worst of all evils, a specimen of American patriotism.

In the crowded square in front of Sleeping Beauty's Castle, a woman sat on a bench reading from a Bible. Not just reading to herself. She was reading out loud, very loudly, aiming the word of God at passersby, who alternately stared in confusion or scattered, steering their strollers into one another to avoid her. I tried to hurry us past the woman, too.

But my boyfriend, a German, was intrigued, and so we stopped to listen. Not once in all my years in Germany did I ever come upon a street evangelist or even meet a Christian, so this must have been, for him, an unusual experience. The woman was reading one of those violent sounding, prophetic passages from Revelation or Daniel or Jeremiah, something about the end of time. She read badly, without the expression and pausing that might have made the words meaningful in the mouth of an orator. Sharon and Tom listened politely, their faces composed into a vague sort of pleasure, as if the woman were just another of the Disney characters that roamed the streets and shook hands with children and crowded into photographs. I was, of course, tortured with shame. Finally, after what seemed like a whole chapter of the woman's flat voice, we moved on. When we were out of earshot, the boyfriend commented that the woman's behavior was ridiculous, so utterly American, and my sister defended her hotly.

"She's just reading her Bible!" she told him—told me too, I could see from her face, even though I was too embarrassed to offer any comment. "She's doing *God's* will, not her own. She doesn't care what other people say."

This was many years before I became a Christian myself, years before I really started thinking about the God of my childhood and my sister's God and wondering whether either God might actually exist. But this image of doing God's will—together with a later, equally embarrassing encounter with college students wearing ties and long skirts dancing in a circle and singing hymns in the middle of Harvard Square—skulked in my memory and became the last stumbling block of my own entry into faith. Even as I lurched from unbelief into the relief of being able to trust my destiny to someone else mightier and smarter and kinder than I was, I worried about that poor woman at Disneyland, those crazed dancers in Harvard Square.

If I became a Christian, I agonized, who knew what lunacy the Lord would expect of me! Would he make me read the Bible before strangers or give everything I owned to the poor and live on the street? Or would it be some worse indignity? Would he send me back to Germany to preach to my friends at drunken dinner parties? And what if I knew it was his will but couldn't make myself do it?

I wouldn't, I decided, be able to do it. I just wasn't humble enough for such embarrassing displays of piety. At thirty, I was too old even for such minor embarrassments as pinning a doily to my hair for mass as I had as a child. I was too intelligent to dance in the street. If God wanted some such feat of faith from me, I'd have to deny him.

Later, when I became a believer, I found Jesus not particularly encouraging on this topic. "[E]veryone who acknowledges me before men," he told his followers, "I also will acknowledge before my Father who is in heaven, but whoever denies me before men, I also will deny before my Father who is in heaven" (Matthew 10:32–33 RSV).

When I was a new Christian, my agitation on this point consumed me, frequently pushing me into unaccustomed acts of mortification. Having noticed some poor fool waving his hands in the air during the singing at church, I made myself join him. I prayed aloud, although doing so always galls me, and once I even went up to the front to lay hands on some newly graduated students we were praying for as a body. During the fellowship time that follows our service, I often forced myself to spend time with people I didn't like or who had nothing to say for themselves, the ones who smiled all the time and had perfect children and always said nice things, people whose very proximity was a trial for me. One day, at work, I offered to pray with a distraught student in my office. And on another occasion, when a fellow teacher wigged out at me in front of our assembled students, I went to her afterward and, swallowing my substantial pride, apologized for having upset her. In short, embarrassing myself became the essence of faith to me.

I remember being impressed as a child with accounts of the saintly living among lepers or with people so profoundly poor that they had no clothes and lived in filth. There were pictures of such people in missionary pamphlets I picked up at church, and just looking at them made me shudder. There could be, I thought back then, nothing more embarrassing than having to live that way, and it amazed me that a person could choose this life, even a nun or a monk devoted to serving God.

I read about how Mother Teresa lived among the poor and the sick in India. She held their heads as they vomited, I remember the report saying. Vomiting, in my child's mind, was the most private and shameful of events. When a child vomited at school, the other children looked away and distanced themselves as much as they could from the sick one. I thought then that there was no greater work of God, no greater embarrassment, than to not only be willingly present while someone vomited but to actually touch them, to hold them while they did it and smell that horrible smell and see the horrid fluid and hear the wretched retching noises. To be truly good was to be like that, I decided even then. To do *God's* will, not one's own. To not worry about what others thought. To not even be bothered by the sight and smell and sound, the sheer intimacy, of vomit, in one's tireless pursuit of God. I think, in my first flush of faith many years later, it was to this child's reverence for shame that I returned. To believe was to be ashamed.

A few years after that, though, my new believer's zealousness wore off, and I lost my some of my original enthusiasm for God's will. Also, I came across another of Jesus' comments that changed everything. The disciples, I learned in John 6:27–29, were worried, as I was, about what it was God wanted of them.

"Do not work for food that spoils," Jesus had been telling them, "but for food that endures to eternal life, which the Son of Man will give you."

But they wanted to know more precisely. "What must we do to do the works God requires?" they demanded.

And Jesus answered them, "The work of God is this: to believe in the one he has sent."

I can't tell you how those words released me, as I'm sure they have released others bound up from childhood in some misconception of godliness that involved doing some terrible task. Faith, I came to think then, frees us from obligatory acts of goodness. And so I gave up embarrassing myself for God entirely and went back to my old ways. If I had some terrible duty before me—some kindness that I was loathe to undertake—I would leave it to God. Do it yourself, I would tell him. Or *make* me do it, if that's your will.

And not much embarrasses me anymore, anyway. This is, I

think, an important by-product of parenting. My daughters have expanded my notion of what my dignity can bear to encompass not merely holding the head of a vomiting person but being thrown up on, in public. I have discovered that I am capable of standing blithely by while one of the girls squats behind a spinner-rack of purses at Wal-Mart to poop in her diaper and of remaining, if not calm, then at least grimly silent, while the other one has a shrieking fit about not getting to have a tiny, hard plastic box of exploding breath mints that costs three dollars.

The other day, on a bus trip, I sat down next to a chatty man in his sixties who had just been dumped by his third wife.

"Is someone sitting here?" I asked him, and he said, no, he was as alone as a person could be.

He had an unusually loud voice, and the people sitting around us all laughed. We were all on our way back to the Orlando airport to fly home after grading Advanced Placement exams for a week at a cavernous Convention Center in Daytona Beach with six hundred other professors and teachers. When the man asked me the inevitable question about where I taught, I lowered my voice and told him the name of the school, and then, when he didn't recognize it, I said it was a private Christian university in Arkansas.

I waited for the usual pause that had followed this announcement all week whenever I got into conversation with someone new. I'm guessing many of my fellow academics there regarded Christian higher education as an oxymoron. Or perhaps it's that something about me—my clothes or the way I talk—failed to prepare them for the fact that I might be a Christian, and they needed a couple of seconds to realign their thoughts. Everyone was too polite to tell me what went on in their heads in that pause, and afterwards, they typically changed the subject.

This man, however, went straight after it.

"You mean, evangelical?" he shouted. He twisted in his seat to stare at me—sternly, it seemed to me—and to see my face when I answered.

I have always been uncomfortable with the term *evangelical,* I need to say here. The adjective it used to be has been bandied around in the media so much of late that the noun *Christian* that it used to modify has been knocked off. Now it's one of those attributive nouns that means something different to whoever uses it.

In the mouths of the people on NPR and on the pages of *Time* and *The Atlantic Monthly,* my primary sources of news and information, the label *evangelical* appears to be synonymous with politically benighted or bigoted or stupid, depending on the context. At best, ridiculously naïve. *Time* has taken to capitalizing the word, which somehow makes it look even more embarrassing. Admitting I *am* one is tantamount to revealing that I am married to a man who spends his free time, together with a bunch of equally besotted men in his model railroad club, decorating expanses of plywood with spray-on grass and watching in glee as miniature locomotives pull empty cars around a circular track to return to where they started out. Worse yet, although I teach at an evangelical college and attend what most would call an evangelical church, whenever I meet fellow Christians who go out of their way to identify themselves as evangelicals, I find myself disagreeing with them on most of their pet subjects. To say I am an evangelical, in my mind, is to be the kind of push-button believer my most arrogant inner self scorns any association with at all.

But, when this stranger asked so directly, so stridently and sternly, some vestige of that old dedication to godly embarrassment rose in my throat and demanded that I admit the truth.

"Yes. Evangelical Christian," I said in my softest possible voice above a whisper. I was sure all of my unseen colleagues around me on the bus were overhearing every word of what we were saying, and I sent up a little prayer—which the Holy Spirit no doubt edited out of my daily offerings to the Father—that the man would dismiss the topic and move on to something less threatening, such as what essay question I had been scoring or whether this was my first time at an AP conference.

"That's great!" he said at the top of his voice and pounded me on the knee. "I'm an evangelical too."

We exchanged names then and more detailed life stories. It turns out that Tom Bateman, raised Catholic like me, was an evangelical Christian in hiding, teaching at a French Christian Brothers boys' high school that had regular masses and required teachers to be Catholic. He had that venom toward his former faith shared by many Catholics who are born-again.

Tom had become an evangelical, as he persisted in calling what we both were, through the ministry of a pastor who arbitrarily visited his hospital room after a stroke had eliminated his peripheral vision, rendering him, as he saw it, helpless, and his life not worth living. After the stroke, he was not only legally blind, but suffering from severe depression. He just wanted, he said, to die. He couldn't drive or do a lot of other things for himself, so his wife had had to do it all, which was one of the several reasons he offered for why she eventually left him. For a while he had clung to the faith of his past life.

"I even got my wife to take me to Québec, to a cathedral there where they have healings all the time. To be healed of my blindness. I believed in miracles then. Still do. Do you?"

Again the stern look and booming voice—like God in my

worst nightmares as a child—demanding that I reveal my most privately held beliefs and acknowledge the most intimate details of my faith before a busload of riveted eavesdroppers, every one of whom I was sure was a sour skeptic.

Healings? Miracles? I could hear them thinking. *Who are these nitwits they let determine the fate of the smartest high school students in the country?*

"Yes. I believe in miracles," I told him. "I believe that people can be healed."

"Well, so we went to this cathedral in Québec," he went on. "It was named after my patron saint. That was another reason I wanted to go there. So, we travel all the way to Canada, which with my wife in charge of arrangements is no small feat. And we get to our hotel and unpack our luggage, and we finally arrive at the cathedral, and the mass is just about to start, and my wife turns to me and says, 'How long is this going to take?'"

For some reason, this struck me as funny, and I laughed. No, I guffawed, if it's possible for a woman to guffaw. I guffawed several times in a row, and then I laughed, and then I guffawed again. Tom looked at me questioningly, and maybe somewhat hurt, and that made it all the funnier.

His blindness wasn't healed, he told me, soberly, but at least he could see well enough to read, and he now traveled extensively on his own. From Orlando, he was headed to China and then Tibet before the semester started back up. He could even drive now, with the aid of special mirrors he fastened onto the regular ones in the car. He pulled one of the mirrors out of his bag to show me and explained how the Department of Motor Vehicles had trained him to constantly check his mirrors against the road as he drove. It was difficult, but it could be done.

I tried to show the appropriate commiseration, but it suddenly seemed a small thing, this blindness of his, made up for by his farseeing faith, which had survived his illness and fear of death and the loss of wives who had once loved him and many other delights of this world he had once loved. In truth, from that story on, everything Tom said struck me as incomparably comical. How he had been disciplined at his school for replacing his students' detention time with taped sermons from famous Christians and gotten kicked out of the daily faculty masses for reading from the Bible and, another time, for offering his own serendipitous prayers out loud during the petitions. Once, during a faculty get-together that opened in prayer, he had prayed for protection against false prophets—from cults and Mormons and such groups, for Muslims, for the lost. Afterwards, a colleague objected.

"Don't you know we Catholics believe in respecting others' faiths?"

"Sure," Tom told him. "And if there were any Mormons present, or Muslims or cult members, I wouldn't have prayed that out loud. But we're all believers in the same thing here, aren't we? Can't we pray openly here from our hearts?"

On another occasion, someone whispered to him during the campus mass, "Aren't you Catholic anymore?" and Tom answered —I imagined him roaring it out above the priest's words and the murmured responses of the congregation—"Am I not here with you?" It sounded like something Jesus himself would say.

By the time we arrived in Orlando, I was laughing so hard that I forgot to worry about the other people on the bus, and when Tom asked me if I would pray with him and grabbed my hand when I agreed, I didn't even flinch.

In the voice of a madman, at the very top of his lungs, he prayed for me—for my work and my family and my soul and the book of spiritual writings I had been working on, that I would find an agent and sell my book. And when it was my turn to pray, I prayed not for the return of his sight as I had been planning to do from the moment he grabbed my hand. I had known, in that moment, that my prayer, his prayer, for renewed sight would be answered if I just prayed it. Instead, though, I prayed that God would find him a wife. Because that was the only real woe that this man had in life, as I saw it: the lack of someone to sit next to him and listen to his stories, someone to accompany him to wherever he went and back home again, to sit beside him as he careened down the road in a car which had a bumper sticker, he told me gleefully, that read, CAUTION! BLIND DRIVER.

"I drive as fast as anyone else," he told me, "but people pretty much keep their distance when they see my sign."

I could see them in my mind. Cars damming up behind him, some veering into the other lanes to screech past him. Their outraged faces. His own amiable smile as he checked now the road before him, now the rear view mirror, now the side mirrors, now the road once more, all the way to his destination.

Relevant and cited scriptural passages: Matthew 10:32–33 and John 6:27–29.

20

Seeing by Faith

The other day I was trying to explain the concept of "voice" to one of my creative writing students whose otherwise strong, concrete, well-crafted writing didn't have one.

"It's like when some guy calls you on the phone and right off starts talking but never says who he is," I told him. "If you don't know the person, the voice means nothing to you. It's just a collection of noises and words. You might be able to gather some facts from what you hear—the caller's approximate age, his place of origin maybe, perhaps his social class or something about why he's calling—but until you recognize the voice, you get no sense of the person behind it."

"In really good writing," I told the student, "we get a sense of a person behind the words on the page, a person we like or commiserate with or disagree with or find funny. When we recognize a voice, we believe in the person it incarnates, and we want to hear more."

I married into the farm community where my husband grew up. Nowadays he's the local CPA, but he used to be a cattle rancher, like most of his clients now and our neighbors. We get a lot of telephone calls from people I don't know, although most callers seem to expect me to know them from the second I hear them on the phone. They're always old. They launch into detailed explanations of problems and needs without ever saying who they are. I guess they think they're locals and have been around so long that even I, someone from another place altogether, ought to recognize their voices by now. Or maybe they think that, since they know *Kris*, I must know *them*.

My kitchen is littered with scraps of paper on which I tried to record the highlights of their messages:

manure spreader?
yesterday
Ruthie said to let you know
723–4180

Often the nameless voice disappears before I manage to extract even a phone number, and I'm left with a worrisome sense of failed responsibility. A confused and elderly woman somewhere mistakenly thinks I'm looking after her. The words I write down are a puzzle for my husband, an urgent message in code that neither of us can decipher:

foreclosure
Chewey Highway
deadline next week
$15 check

Sometimes they irk me, these callers.

"But who are you?" I interject into the stream of crisis upon crisis, need upon need. The question flusters them even more.

"Oh, Kris will know," they tell me finally, confident and wrong, stupidly wrong, and I have to consciously edit the sourness from my voice: "No. He won't. Not unless I can tell him your name."

I hear the contours of the phone voice: its highs and lows, its desperation, its trust in my husband, in me even, a stranger, to attend to some dire task. But I can't see the person behind the words. I can't connect the voice to a face, a name, a story. Sometimes—it shames me to say it—I reject the caller even as I listen for words to write down. I don't pay attention. Or I write nothing. I cut the call short. And later I rail to my eighty-year-old mother-in-law about the local lack of phone etiquette.

Occasionally, after the third or fourth call from the same distraught stranger, I get mean and feign ignorance. "Now, who did you say you are?" I demand, making the poor old geezer say all of it all over again: the name, the problem, the phone number, the time it's best to call.

I'm like this with God, too. When he calls—which he does continually, although I am frequently away from the phone—I hear the things he says but usually forget or neglect or even refuse to recognize the person behind the voice. I read the words on the pages of my Bible and forget to acknowledge the patient, holy, just, loving, lovesick person they incorporate, to see in my mind those familiar invisible qualities behind the pressing matters of creation that so consume me.

Seeing by faith requires, I think, an intentional refocusing of our ordinary sight, a conscious recognition of the person of God behind everything we see and hear and smell and feel and taste. Looking at the world through the eyes of faith takes everything I usually lack when those old voices call: patience, humility, respect, conscious goodwill, genuine love for those in need, for my neighbor. To see by faith is to search out and lay claim to these invisible qualities found even in ourselves—creatures made in God's image—qualities hidden deep within us in the safe cleft of his grace and provision.

Which is not to fault God's phone manners, I may need to clarify. I mean, we need to respect him as a local guy who's been around awhile.

Relevant and cited scriptural passages: Genesis 1:26–27 and Romans 1:18–20.

21

My Naomi

My seventy-something-year-old mother-in-law stayed in the room with me throughout my labor with my first child. It may have been that she felt obliged to be there to play her own mother's role as makeshift midwife in the country community where she grew up. Or she may have been motivated by some more basic urge to see her only son's progeny into the world—to tickle the baby's nostrils with a blade of grass, as we used to do to a newborn calf when we had to help its mama with a difficult delivery. In any case, she was there, doused in Prince Matchabelli perfume, as she always is when she goes out in public, exclaiming over my contractions displayed on the fetal monitor and chatting with the doctor about my progress.

It seemed natural to me at the time for her to be there, even though my mother-in-law and I were not close then and, when I wasn't moaning, I was wishing she'd leave. I didn't even have a name for her that I felt comfortable using in those days. With my own mother only recently dead, I couldn't bring myself to call her Mom. She was and still is known around where we live by two names—Anna for strangers and Texie for intimates—but I wasn't ever sure to which group I properly belonged as the stranger who had married her son.

Later, after Charlotte was born and could laugh and roll over onto her belly and hold things tightly in her fist, my mother-in-law became Mamaw, the local name for a grandmother that was one of Charlotte's first words. But in the early days of my marriage, before Charlotte and even a little while after she was born, my relationship with my mother-in-law was fraught with avoidance. Although we saw each other every day on the farm, we avoided naming each other, touching each other, genuinely conversing, or even looking at each other. With my husband and her son between us, we were like two balls on a string twisted into orbit: clacking violently, unwillingly together, then parting as suddenly.

Life on the farm truly is about family. I didn't realize this until it was too late and I was part of it. My new husband and I lived in the little three room house my husband had grown up in before his parents built the ranch house across the street where my mother-in-law still lives. We farmed the land he had in joint tenancy with her after his father's death. We saw his mother a dozen times a day. We stored our farm tools in her garage, ate swift meals at her kitchen bar between haying tasks, shared with her the outdoor clothes she hung on a hook next to the door to her utility room. If it started raining and we were in the hayfield, she drove out in the pick-up to rescue us from potential lightening. On hot afternoons she would stride out into the field with a cool drink for my tea-aholic husband, the glass carefully tented with aluminum foil against flies. She would have brought me one, too, but I always abstained. What I wanted in those early days of my marriage was privacy, solitude shared with the man I had married, and the reassurance that I, not his mother, could fulfill his needs. Coming from Southern California and a dysfunctional family, I had no memory of such closeness to one's kin, and it seemed sick to me. *Enmeshed* is what my psychology friends called it.

Later, when I was a new Christian, the leader of my Bible study group told me to get over it. She was from a similarly close family. She told me that my mother-in-law's smothering participation in our life and my husband's acquiescence to it were the normal and in fact necessary behavior of farm families. Farm families need their parents to get it all done, she said. *So much for leave and cleave*, I thought.

It *was* becoming increasingly difficult to get it all done, though, especially after we had Charlotte. Mamaw took care of the baby while we did the daily chores. Charlotte would be wailing with hunger by the time I was able to rush in and nurse her, and Mamaw would shush her as I undid my coveralls and settled myself on a stool at the bar.

"Here now," she cooed. "The jugs are coming. The jugs are coming."

Soon cattle prices plummeted, and I took a job "in town," as farmers call the off-farm jobs farmwives usually have to do to make family farming possible these days. Having taught college English before my marriage, I got alternatively certified to teach grades seven through twelve and took a position at a nearby school. Public school education is the hardest work I have ever done—not comparable in the least to the college level teaching I had done previously. The seventh graders were demonic, and the high school students were like some sort of poisonous slug, sticky and noncompliant and, though boneless, somehow capable of the most powerful resistance to being moved that I have ever encountered.

We built a new house with money Mamaw lent us, although she refused to call it lending, refused to talk about it at all. What was hers was ours, she said. By then I had another baby, Lulu, and, by the time I arrived at Mamaw's house after school to pick up my daughters, I was too exhausted to enjoy them dragging me from room to room to show me things and climbing all over me in their happiness to see me.

When the girls and I got home, I would change clothes while they pretended to help me make dinner with their doll dishes, spreading butter and crumbs and sugar everywhere. And somewhere in all of this Kris would come in from the farmwork, and Mamaw would call and tell us what she had made for dinner and that there was enough for us, even though she knew we were planning to eat at home, and often we would eat down at her house after all just because there were still dishes in the sink from breakfast, and I needed to grade papers, and everything was so hectic.

I was resentful toward Mamaw, and embarrassed to be resentful toward someone to whom I was so indebted. She raised my children, opened gates for my husband in my absence, provided us with a house. My Bible study leader told me I should let her cook for us and just be thankful.

She didn't understand that cooking, for me, has always been a pleasure, not a chore. As an eight-year-old child, I had taken over all the cooking for my family of eight. That made the kitchen my haven from the chaos of my feuding brothers and sisters and angry parents. No one was allowed to come in while I was cooking, and they had to eat what I served. And, having performed my duty, I alone of my sisters could leave the table as soon as the meal was over, while they still had dishes to wash. Eating at Mamaw's meant surrendering one of my most precious retreats from the difficulties of life, my escape and solitude, my self-made and hard-won identity as the provider of food for my family.

I was meanwhile progressing as a Christian, though. I had taken upon me a plan of reading sequentially through the Bible for the first time. I had previously read here and there and enjoyed the stories of many Bible characters as a child—notably Jonah, who wouldn't do what God told him to; Martha, who wanted her sister to help her with the housework; and Peter, who walked on water and then suddenly noticed the waves and started to sink. So, much of what I read in the early books of the Bible was at least vaguely familiar to me.

When I got to the story of Ruth and her mother-in-law Naomi though, I couldn't remember ever reading it—perhaps it wasn't included in our children's Bible—but I did recognize in Ruth's words a song I liked that we had sung in church when I was little:

Wherever you go, I shall go.
Wherever you live, there shall I live.
Your people will be my people,
and your God will be my God, too.

Even if as a child I had known the story of Ruth joining forces with her mother-in-law, I couldn't have had any idea back then, long before my marriage, what such a realignment of allegiances might have entailed. But now, as a new Christian and a newcomer in my community and a wife struggling for my place in a new family, the story of Ruth's relationship with her mother-in-law alarmed me considerably. *Was this how I was supposed to feel?* I wondered. *Why didn't I? Was I wrong to resist my mother-in-law's involvement in my life, her nurturing, her insistence on providing for our needs? Or, as my non-Christian friends insisted, was my mother-in-law overstepping her territory?*

Ruth's husband, I reminded myself, was dead, so she would have had fewer options than a woman in our time and culture. Manless, she had to take what shelter she could find—even if it meant embracing her mother-in-law's race and rituals, embracing her mother-in-law herself. But I knew that there was something deeper than opportunism behind Ruth's pledge, some more honorable impulse, some more selfless sort of love than I knew how to practice that led her to take up with her mother-in-law and renounce where she was from and who she was and, most amazing of all, what she believed in.

Long before my marriage, I came across the writings of Maxie Wander, an East German writer who captured the voices of a variety of East German women in her edited transcriptions of their stories in a book entitled *Guten Morgen, Du Schöne* (*Good Morning, Beautiful*). In the collection was the account of a young bride during the Second World War whose husband had left for the front just days after their marriage. She barely knew him, and yet, without money or prospects or even the most modest means of survival, she left her home in the city for the countryside where he was from. There, she took up residence with her new mother-in-law, a tough self-made woman, the archetypal peasant wife of folk tales, the kind who cuts her own wood and sells livestock and is considerably wiser and more stoic than her numskull of a husband.

Like Mamaw and like Naomi, the mother-in-law in Wander's book is a widow and inseparable from her daughter-in-law's new life. In the face of widespread hunger throughout Germany, the two of them have to plant and harvest and butcher their own food, and the younger city woman learns all these skills from the older country woman. They both have to work hard to survive. In point of fact, neither could probably have made it without the other, but in the daughter-in-law's bright voice I hear no bitterness or even consciousness of hardship. Instead, I hear the voice of Ruth, the voice of a person impossibly loving, impossibly thankful, impossibly unconscious of her own goodness, her own contribution to their continued existence.

My Naomi is small and wiry and relentlessly healthy. When Charlotte and Lulu were little, they affectionately introduced her to new acquaintances as "the seventy-eight-year-old"—or whatever her current age was at the time—but they never considered her old. When they learned to differentiate "children" from "adults," they included Mamaw with the children, and even today, in her mid-eighties, she seems young. She climbed trees with the girls until they grew out of it. She walks miles through the woods early every morning, before even my husband and I are up, although we rise at five or five-thirty. She ricks her own woodpile and, in wintertime, hauls in armfuls of logs daily to stoke up the fire in what she calls her "insert," a sooty glass chamber enclosing her fireplace with fans to blow the heat out into the house.

She spells out the letters of words that are foreign or that she thinks she can't pronounce, rather than risk pronouncing them incorrectly. She votes religiously—calling me up to remind me that its Election Tuesday—and steadfastly refuses to reveal who or what she voted for. "Voting is a privilege, and each person should vote his own way and not be influenced by anyone else," Mamaw has explained to me more than once. She gets mad when certain old ladies call her when she's cooking or playing with the girls, and she calls them that—old ladies—as if she is not one herself.

Her idea of a good meal is a tomato with about two tablespoons of cottage cheese, for which she uses the plural pronoun "they," as in, "They were just what I was hungry for with that tomato." She has an enormous summer garden and is much attached to her collection of yard and garden implements: she owns and uses two mowers, three tillers, and countless trimmers and sprayers and other tools. When there's a skunk or an armadillo around her house, she gets out her .22 pistol and shoots it.

She buys local but banks across the state-line, in Arkansas, where it doesn't matter to her as much if the people know how much money she has. She has always balanced her own checkbook, and when she gets her social security check in the mail she makes sure they withheld the correct amount. She records the weather and the key events of her life on a calendar in her utility room: when Lulu and Charlotte lost each tooth, when Kris passed the CPA exam and what his score was, when I went on trips and where I went. Recently, when Charlotte had to do a timeline of her life for school, Mamaw got out her old calendars, and there it all was, every event Charlotte thought was important and many more she would never have remembered.

Ordinarily loud, Mamaw lowers her voice to pray over our shared meals, and she always asks God to forgive her sins, even though, as my children have pointed out, she is just supposed be saying thank you for the food. Whenever I ask her why she does something the way she does, she invariably says, "That's just the way we've always done it." Once Mamaw gave me the top of a carrot that she had kept in a saucer of water on her window sill until it shot up a froth of lacy yellow-green leaves.

Hers is the fiber from which whole cloth is made, an inspiration for any would-be Ruth or striving Christian, a model of selfless love of herself, others, and life itself. As I get older and more sure of the choices I have made, for better or for worse, I begin to see how one might come to cling to such a pillar in time of need. I already cling to her, in fact. More and more, when time is short and stressful, I seek her ease, her meals, her love for my children and attention to their demands.

My old friends tell me I speak her language now. I cook the kinds of things she likes to eat—chicken and dumplings, biscuits, cole-slaw—and I pronounce words with a slight but perceptible Oklahoma accent. Often I go to her house just to sit at the bar and drink a cup of watery coffee that she complains is too strong and to hear a rendition, repeated several times over, of exactly what each of my daughters has eaten at her house that day and to read the newspaper, from which she sets aside the sections she knows I like or an article about something she's sure will interest me. Although sometimes it irritates me, I take a distinct pleasure in knowing what I will find when I get to her house. I suppose I have become enmeshed.

Relevant and cited scriptural passages: Ruth, Jonah, Matthew 14:22–33, and
    Luke 10:38–41.
Other references:
Maxie Wander. *Guten Morgen, Du Schöne.* Berlin (GDR): Luchterhand, 1977.
"Wherever You Go." Gregory Norbet and the monks of Weston Priory.
    Benedictine Foundation of the State of Vermont. 1972.

22

Erasure

Early in my marriage, I went to visit my grandparents in Arkansas. Although I had settled down in the nearby state of Oklahoma, I am ashamed to say I only visited them a handful of times before they died. I could offer the excuse that the new busy-ness of my life kept me from traveling much in those days, and this would be true. Somehow, from the moment I had babies, not only did my travels end, but my desire to travel was suddenly engulfed in such a sea of child-related concerns—diaper bags, motion sickness, quadrupled plane fares, passports, finding restaurants suitable for children, making reservations for lodging when in the past I just got rooms on the fly—that I knew I had to give the traveling up. But to say that this is why I neglected my grandparents would be a lie.

It wasn't the distance, either. I did live six hours away, but that was closer to them than anyone else in my family. Closer to them than to many of my friends whom I would have dropped everything to visit had they been, as my grandparents always were, in ill health.

No, it was a different distance that kept me away. It was the distance of age and economy and class that separated us. Of culture. Of self-centered priorities. Of my persistent inability to embrace the misery of such a visit. My grandparents were aging and poor and hard to talk to. They came from another world than any of the worlds I was familiar with—a world characterized by spittoons and fried fatback and trash burning in the yard. Skunks under the floorboards. Missing teeth. Canasta. The cessation of activity that was their life made me notice the whir of crickets in the air, it's true. But it also made me fidget for the day to end, for the last domino to be laid, six to six, next to the ring of water pooling around my glass of sweet tea on the table. From the moment I arrived, I could hardly wait for the time to come when it might not be rude to say I had to go back home to my girls.

Whenever I went to see my grandparents, they insisted on chauffeuring me around—sometimes to places hours away—to visit other relatives I had never heard of. Aunt Myrtie. Jess and Bess. Rosalie—"She's your cousin, you know." Often whoever it was lay in the hospital, yellow and skinny and round-bellied from cancer, surrounded by more relatives I had never heard of. Other times, we went to someone's house, usually a house just like my grandparents' house: the same wood floors and spittoons, the same vinyl-backed curtains holding in the airlessness, the same wheeze of crickets beyond the door.

Once, my grandparents took me to visit a distant uncle whose wife had recently died. He had weeks before moved in with his son and his wife—both cousins of mine, evidently, although they were as old as my parents—and they had just found out that the old man was in the latter stages of Alzheimer's disease. He'd been forgetting the names of things and acting befuddled for quite some time, but his wife had always managed to cover up for him, and the changes in his behavior occurred so slowly that the family didn't really notice that he had a problem until he was living in the house with them. Now the uncle had to have someone with him at all times. He was often upset because he regarded the entire family as mean strangers trying to get him to do things that made no sense to him. Nevertheless, he didn't like it when they left him alone, and he wasn't happy unless he was right in the middle of what they were doing.

"Who are you?" he would ask. "What's happening to me? Where am I?" Like my mother in the last years of her life, he was perpetually lost.

The son and daughter-in-law were country people. They had what my mother-in-law calls an Old MacDonald's farm—a chaotic clutch of animals and chores and broken machinery that enabled their survival, but just barely. They were the sere, independent people one sees in Grant Wood paintings. Resigned to difficulty and illness. Immune, somehow, to worry. Like the people I am surrounded with in Oklahoma.

Our Oklahoma neighbors never talk about family matters. They might show up on our farm—or we on theirs—to help out if we have hay down and about to get rained on, and we might exchange a few neutral words about a broken tractor and a field to plow, or a cow that has escaped to the road or is having trouble calving. Whoever has the trouble has to interrupt the ensuing frenzy—doubling the windrows so as to put up the hay faster or getting parts before shops closed or locating the necessary tools— to just stand around with the neighboring farmer, who shows up out of nowhere to commiserate or troubleshoot or just find out what's going on.

"Think it might be that bearing, huh? Went out last year about this time, too, if I recall. Probably won't make it to the shop before it closes. Maybe need to go out to Doug's? It's closer, anyway. Probably won't have one, though." Meanwhile, the rain has arrived, or the shop has in fact closed, or the cow has limped off to who knows where in the woods.

Illness in the family is a private matter in the country, a matter of taking care of one's own, of longsuffering, which is always practiced in privacy and silence. I'm relatively new to this country way of thinking. Having been raised in suburbia, I grew up thinking matters of business—such as farm work—were private matters. I never knew how much money my own dad made or exactly what he did at his job as an aeronautical engineer. If he were having problems at work or, God forbid, financial trouble, our neighbors would have been the last to know about it. Family illness, however, was a public event. One announced one's own or a loved one's infirmity to friends and even strangers, preparing them for whatever divergence from normal behavior the infirmity might bring with it.

"This is my mom," we used to say to newcomers to our household. "She had a brain tumor removed and has no short-term memory, so she'll forget your name as soon as you say it."

Californians suffering from illness or disabilities attended support groups of fellow sufferers. There were even support groups for the family of the one suffering. When people we knew learned of my mother's illness, they typically had advice to offer.

"She's suffering from dementia, huh? My mom's the same. We've got her in a nursing home out in Long Beach. Bet that's what you'll have to do pretty soon here. Might try the one in Santa Ana. It's closer, anyway. Might not take people with dementia, though."

There are no Alzheimer's support groups out in the country in

Oklahoma—or out in the countryside of Arkansas. When I brought the topic up with the uncle's son and daughter-in-law—that they might want to find such a group—they looked alarmed. They were too embarrassed to discuss the old man's problem with me openly, and they seemed to think my probing questions heartless.

I told them that my mom had had dementia, too, although hers was from brain surgery, but this only confused matters.

"But he's got Old-Timer's," the wife told me, "not that other thing." Then she changed the subject for the third or fourth time. They would not talk about it, could not talk about it. The old man's illness was whispered news, not something to talk openly about with a stranger, especially a stranger like this one, cousin or not, with her big words and bold ways. Illness was not a subject for troubleshooting.

Nevertheless, I did what any Southern Californian would do when faced with a crisis: I told them about a self-help book I had read that taught the ins and outs of dealing with dementia. I still had it at home, and it gave lots of practical advice, such as, if you're washing dishes, give your loved one with dementia a towel and some dishes, too, and let him wipe at them and stack them in another dish rack while you work. I offered to send them the book when I got home.

The wife was perplexed.

"But I only have one dish rack," she said. "And he'll break a dish if you give him one."

"Give him plastic ones. Just go out and get cheap stuff at Wal-Mart," I told her.

She looked back at me with the bleakest expression I ever saw on anyone's face. Clearly, she could not believe that this cousin from Oklahoma—or California, or Germany, or wherever it was she said she came from—was recommending she buy another dish rack and set of dishes to solve her father-in-law's little problem.

The old man, however, looked anything but bleak. He sat on the couch in the living room playing with a string. His shiny face wore the same blissful expression my mom's always wore in the years following her surgery until she died eleven years later. Despite occasional fits of paranoia and annoyance, she looked incomparably happy, happier than she had ever looked in the years she spent raising my five siblings and me.

It was a happiness that came from release. I know this. To this day I fantasize about being terminally ill. In my fantasies, there is no pain. There are no worries or deadlines, no work sitting at the back of my mind waiting to be caught up on, nothing I want to write but don't have the time for, no essays to grade. In my fantasies, time—the little time available to me before I die—expands into a miniature eternity, in which every concern I previously had is erased, eradicated, turned into peace and serenity, into my mother's crazy blissful smile.

The other day my division chair, Terri, called to tell me to put her on our division's prayer list because her computer was down, and she was frantic. They had given her some sort of ersatz computer on which to conduct e-mail business, but it used a system foreign to her, and she was lost.

Her voice sounded like my brain does most of the time, like the mass of stuffing and yarn and embroidery thread in my sewing box from which my daughters are always asking me to separate out a certain color for some project that has to be done right now.

"You're just going to have to wait," I tell them, spreading the mass out between my fingers, trying to elucidate the path of magenta through the greens and yellows and reds and wads of polyester stuffing. "I don't know how everything got all mixed up like this."

But it has always been messed up that way and probably always will be. Sometimes I fantasize about throwing it all out and buying all new colors of embroidery thread and yarn and keeping them, somehow, in their little paper collars, or perhaps in baggies, one to a color.

Anyway, I forwarded Terri's prayer request in an e-mail to our division members and added what seemed a relevant scripture I had noticed that morning in Ecclesiastes:

Consider what God has done:
Who can straighten
what he has made crooked?
When times are good, be happy;
but when times are bad, consider:
God has made the one
as well as the other. (7:13–14)

I guess I was thinking, *Who can fix the computer God has broken?* Or something like that. Poor Terri did not reply, and a few days after her call, my division received this e-mail message from her:

Guys, I would appreciate your continued prayers. I got the computer back this afternoon with the info that I had lost everything. There was no way to retrieve anything. Unfortunately I have not been backing up anything for the past several years and everything is gone.

She went on to encourage us to back up our own hard drives onto the network.

But it was lost. Gone. Irretrievable. I felt like a cad for having suggested that God had had a hand in it.

I've been thinking about Terri's e-mail. Her advice, which I have been meaning to follow but haven't gotten around to, woke me up last night.

I need to remember to back up my computer, I earnestly reminded myself, concentrating on the doorknob of the bedroom, dimly visible in the darkness, to turn the worry into a post-hypnotic suggestion. Then, before I could talk myself back to sleep, I thought of the tangled mass of stuff on my computer hard drive. Assignments and revisions of assignments. Essays, some finished and some years later still in progress. Final exams, each with its own password to open. Old emails from people I had forgotten about. Advertisements for conferences I had attended long in the past. *I ought to sort it all out,* I thought, *throw out whatever is unnecessary and only keep what I have to have.*

And what would that be? What, exactly, of all this jumble of stuff, was essential? I started to list it in my head, sorting it into imaginary folder icons. I made a few rules about cut off dates. *Nothing older than a year, unless it's my own writing. Or unless it's really important and I just know I'll forget it. Or unless . . .*

It was no use. The more I thought of it, the more tangled my mind got, and the less likely I was to fall back asleep. I ended up having to fantasize about languishing in the hospital without hope of ever reemerging well and whole. Every once in a while, some stranger would come and wash me or turn me over or adjust the tubes that kept me fed.

On the morning Terri called me, another sentence from the same chapter of Ecclesiastes had struck me:

Do not say, "Why were the old days better than these?"
For it is not wise to ask such questions. (7:10)

Why was it not wise? I wondered at the time. Did it mean the old days were really not better than these? That all that information on Terri's computer—and on mine—was better off lost? That the old uncle was better off not knowing where he was and what was happening to him? That my mother, trapped in the immediate present, had been more fortunate than we? That her blissful smile held a truth that even the wise could not fathom?

One of my colleagues in the biblical studies division of my university recently told me that the middle part of Ecclesiastes, where I had been reading, amounted to "the wrongheaded theological musings of some wisdom tradition in Israel, probably not Solomon," and that only the prologue and epilogue represent what he called "normative theology."

I love the book of Ecclesiastes because it contains such practical advice on jobs and stress and spiritual prioritization. It's a sort of biblical self-help book that I find much more applicable to our time than many other passages of scripture. I recommend it often to my students and reread certain sections myself whenever I feel like I'm letting conflicts at work or my worries about my children or problems with students get all mixed up with what's really important in my life: my relationship with my creator and savior. I like it because it reminds me of certain truths only my gut can appreciate for what they are, truths like obsession, duty, bliss. Ecclesiastes, the teacher, whoever he was, knew something important about life—how it catches us up in its fibrous activity, how we can't get free no matter how relentlessly we sort and struggle, how we aren't even capable of genuinely wanting loose. We are like the Israelites, lingering for a generation at that mountain on the border of the Promised Land.

Christian novelist Flannery O'Connor, who struggled throughout her adult life with lupus and eventually died of it at age thirty-nine, once said she felt sorry for those who did not suffer serious illness, which she described in a letter to a friend as "one of God's mercies." Her own illness involved pain and disfigurement, which I would not want to suffer. Nevertheless, I think I know what she meant. Actively knowing one is going to die, and probably sooner than one had been planning on, must be such a relief. How else can we get our minds around that wonderful, awful truth: that we are not in charge?

Relevant and cited scriptural passages: Ecclesiastes, especially chapter 7.
Other references:
Flannery O'Connor. *The Habit of Being: Letters of Flannery O'Connor.* Sally
    Fitzgerald, ed. New York: Vintage, 1980. (p.163).

23

On Moving Mountains

The other morning I learned from the radio that mountains move. I caught the tail end of a National Public Radio account about a cartographer who charts their movement. Mount Everest, he said, is traveling toward China at a rate of a few centimeters a year. It was an interesting idea. I thought of all those Chinese people I met when I lived there whose life work seemed to be finding a way out of China. The Chinese were moving out; the mountains were moving in, I mused. An intriguing picture of entropy in reverse.

"That's the beauty of mountains," the cartographer reveled behind my thoughts. "They're always moving."

Then he quoted what he called "the great German philosopher Goethe," saying something to the effect that if you think you can do something impossible, you should go ahead and try. It sounded like a slogan for the Marines, I thought, although a bit too wordy. Evidently the cartographer's measuring of mountain movement, which involved an Everest expedition from what I could gather, was thought impossible before he tried it.

Of course, I started thinking right then about what the great Jewish philosopher Jesus had to say about moving mountains and achieving the impossible.

"I tell you the truth," he told his disciples, who were despondent about their failure to drive a demon from a boy who was having seizures, "if you have faith as small as a mustard seed, you can say to this mountain, 'Move from here to there' and it will move. Nothing will be impossible for you" (Matthew 17:20–21).

For a moment I thought that the cartographer's words represented yet another example for the faithless modern listener that scientists or doctors or psychologists—or, in other words, people, not God—were in control. Why seek a healer when medicines can do the trick? they seem to always be saying. Why look for a spiritual solution to what was obviously a material problem? I remembered the Apollo 13 astronaut I'd heard speak about the crew saving themselves from certain death through their own ingenuity. Why seek a savior if we can save ourselves?

Having not heard the beginning of the NPR broadcast, I can't be certain there wasn't some argument offered that humans and their doings were causing the mountain movement, but I assume that it is the result of geological conditions beyond our control—some shifting of plates or the fact that mountains are floating like croutons on a soup of molten earth. So the cartographer wasn't talking about succeeding in the impossible task of actually moving mountains by his own efforts but merely measuring their movement.

I have moved a lot in my life. I had thought about that, too, earlier in the morning as I read an account in, the *Wall Street Journal* of a family very like the one I grew up in, except apparently healthy. A lengthy and engaging history of the Fiedler family is noteworthy enough to be in the *Wall Street Journal* because of the fact that four of six kids in the family are CEO's or presidents of major companies. They got there, according to journalist Matt Murray, because of a nightly habit of arguing at the dinner table, emphasis on independence and individuality, and teamwork.

Told in scenes of family life, the article could have been describing my family but for its cheery and affirmative tone and the fact that none of us became CEO's. The nightly dinner table argument, replete with the Fiedlers "interrupting and finishing one another's sentences" as at my house, actually sounded fun, despite Matt Murray's violent verb choices, like *lob* and *rage*, for what all went on.

"'It was kind of like *Crossfire* at dinnertime,'" one of the future CEOs remarked with tender nostalgia. And afterwards, "'everyone would walk up from the table and go play golf or something.'"

As in my family, the highest goal in the Fiedler family was success for its own sake. The father of the family disparagingly pointed out quitters to the children as they were growing up so that they knew, as one family member put it, "you never wanted to hear him say that about you." In my family, whenever one of us got cranky in a game or an argument, whenever one of us was a poor sport and sniffed out some dismissive statement like, "I don't really care if I win or not," my dad would show up from nowhere and boom, "Show me someone who doesn't want to win, and I'll show you a loser!"

Like the Fiedlers, we were encouraged to work as soon as we were able. At twelve I cleaned houses and babysat at a resort. From that point on I bought all my own clothes. At fifteen, as soon as I could drive, I lied my way into a job at a bookstore in the mall, where I worked thirty hours a week for the next six years as a department manager while I finished high school and graduated cum laude from the nearby University of California. Then I left. I left home for New Orleans, then Boston, then Berlin, then Beijing, then Hong Kong, then Arkansas, and finally rural Oklahoma, where I married, had kids, and now live.

My movement all over the world, I thought this morning during the quiet time my husband and I share before our daughters get up, was my faithless attempt to control my fate, to do the impossible and to be content in spite of the miseries of my growing-up years. Like the scientists and doctors of today, I thought that I could save and heal myself. By sheer will I could shed ugliness and loss and pain and leave it all behind me. I could be a better person. I could stop hurting.

Just now I looked up *fate* and *faith* in my *American Heritage Dictionary* to see if they had the same etymological roots. I wanted to be able to say, "Guess what? They do!" They don't, though. They are, in fact, near opposites. *Faith* comes from the Latin *fides,* which means the same thing, while *fate* comes from the Latin *fatum,* the past participle of the verb *to speak.* Hmm. Say the impossible, and that makes it happen. Faith is trust in what we can't see; fate is trust in our ability to say it true.

The other day, a perky student from my undergraduate alma mater back in California called to solicit money from me as an alumna. I was in the final half hour of cooking a meal for the eleven students in my creative writing course.

"We want to know about you," she told me. "What do you do now?" I stretched the phone cord across the kitchen to stir the pot of butter beans with jowl meat, turn on the rice steamer, and strew one last layer of smashed garlic and rosemary on the roasting chicken.

I told her I teach English at a nearby college.

"Wow," she told me, "that sounds hard."

Get to the point, I told her in my mind; *I don't have time to chat.* The tablecloths were upstairs in the linen closet, and I needed to iron one before my guests got there.

"Well," she chattered on, "what kind of advice could you give to someone like me about getting a job after college?"

"I don't really know," I told her, squeezing the receiver carefully against my shoulder as I tried to extend the table with my garlicky fingertips. "It kind of depends on what you want to do." I got the table leaves out of the pantry and looked at the clock. It's so hard to establish boundaries with people on the phone.

"Well, how did you get your job as a professor?" she wanted to know.

I thought about the little advertisement for a position at a nearby Christian university that a colleague had interrupted my chaotic high school English class to give me, about how official transcripts and letters of recommendation and statements of faith had to be assembled and received by the week's end, and about the unlikely interview that had lasted all day and required that I give a sample lecture to a class of students I had never seen before. I thought about how I love teaching now because I'm not spending my effort and time and ingenuity controlling unbelievably wild high school classes and filling out forms for the State Department of Education and worrying about kids growing up with present lives far more desperate than my past. Instead, I teach willing students how to seize their faith in their writing.

"How did I get my job? God put me in it," I told her, knowing that this wasn't what she wanted to hear. I could smell the garlic browning in the oven.

"Oh," she said. She was silent a moment. Then, "You mean fate?"

"No, God," I told her with conviction. "God put me here."

"Oh, well, whatever," she said now, sounding suddenly smug and dismissive and much older and more tired than before.

She sounded like I used to feel, I thought. As if she had been pushing and pushing and pushing at a mountain, knowing she could move it, if she just set her mind to it, but getting nowhere. I wanted to touch her, hug her. I would have invited her to dinner had she not been so far away.

Not long after I figured out the connection between hope and faith and began to believe, I became enamored of a verse from Deuteronomy: "You have stayed long enough at this mountain," God told the Israelites at Horeb (1:6). They had been wandering around the desert for years and years, reluctant to cross the Jordan and claim the land that he had promised them. I felt that I had lingered too long at my mountain—pushed on it, leaned on it, worshipped it, run away from it and back to it my whole life long—and it was time now to quit thinking I could budge it on my own. God has spoken this verse to me over and over again since then, every time I get to thinking I run the show.

Mountains move, I've finally come to realize, but God does it. He just flicks our mountains out of the way when we lay claim to his promises. And our lives after that are merely a measure of the movement.

Relevant and cited scriptural passages: Deuteronomy 1:6, Matthew 17:20–21, and Hebrews 11:1.
Other references:
"Mount Everest." *Morning Edition*. NPR. KUAF, 12 November 1999.
Matt Murray. "Bred to Rise: Leon and Betty Fiedler Reared a Brood Geared for Corporate Success." *Wall Street Journal*. 10 November 1999, A.1.

24

Learning How to Honor

T he other day my therapist gave me the assignment to figure out how to honor my own needs in a problem situation we had been discussing. I was intimidated by a total stranger on a committee I had recently been invited to join. He was a man the size of a mountain with a booming voice and large, condescending gestures. He leaned so far back from our little table that he was almost reclining, hands clasped across his stomach—like the scary principal in a movie or your dad when he's found you out. From this remote stance he regarded us—me in particular, it seemed—through half open eyes. He grimaced dismissively whenever anyone made a suggestion. He didn't know me, but I felt as though he did, as though he had known me for a long time and had looked deep into me and found me wanting.

When I say intimidated, I don't mean the ordinary small and stupid kind of intimidated, but rather the frantic, uncontrollable kind that could turn into tears. I was, in short, terrified of the man. Something about him had triggered a panic attack in me, I figured out afterward, and I was trying to decide between quitting the committee or coming up with a way to deal with him, when my therapist told me the problem was not about the committee or the man but about me, about what I needed to get out of it all.

"For next time," he said, "think about what your needs are on this committee and how you might honor them."

You need to know, first of all, that *honor* is my therapist's favorite word. Whenever I reveal some minor atrocity of my life, he tells me he is *honored* to be told it. He always says he is *honored* when I read him something I have written. And now this business of figuring out how to *honor* my needs.

At first it bugged me when I noticed he used this word all the time. I always hate it when someone becomes predictable. Also, not having been raised in the habit of being told anything I did honored anyone—which is a big part of the problem that acquainted me with my therapist in the first place—I wasn't really sure what he meant by it. It was such a formal word. I couldn't remember ever using it myself. I guessed it might be therapist lingo for, "Okay, I gotcha. Let's move on." Or, worse, a works-for-anything response to the blurted out horrors he must have to deal with hourly.

After the first couple of times he used the word but before it started to irritate me, I got to thinking maybe I should try it out next time one of my students or friends told me something really awful. I'm always looking for a good hedge that gives me time to get my thoughts in order.

But, when the first opportunity came up, I couldn't get the words out. My friend Imogene's husband Jackie started telling me about how he couldn't talk to his wife about even positive things the cancer doctor said to him—like that, in checking her broken shoulder, he found no physical indication that her cancer had spread there—because it made the possibility of her dying too real to him. I knew I was hearing what he had told few others, not even Imogene herself, and I was grasping for something to say, some way to comfort him, but telling him that I was honored to know about his pain simply would not come out of my mouth. I said nothing. I just felt bleak. And Jackie looked even bleaker. His light blue eyes teared up. He turned away from me to deposit a flat of eggs from their hen houses on my counter and gather up the bag of homemade chicken pot pies he had come for, and then he left.

A couple of months into my therapy, I stopped being peeved whenever my therapist said the h-word and even started kind of liking it. It seemed to sum him up, somehow: a quiet man who feels honored by and honors others. It was a good way to be, I thought—generally respectful of others and serious-minded about their troubles. It comforted me to think of him like that.

Once, when I was a graduate student, one of my professors remarked that I always use the word *problematic*—in my speaking and in my writing. I told the professor that the word *problematisch* was a really ordinary word in Germany, where I had been living, and that that was how I got in the habit of using it, which was true, but in retrospect I think I embraced the word because it sort of sums me up. I'm problematic.

So then I get this assignment to honor my own needs, and I'm thinking, *Honor, what is honor? How can I honor something if I don't even know what that entails?* I mean, I kind of knew what the word meant, but I didn't know how to do it. Being told to "honor my own needs" was like being told to "just give my worries to Jesus." I have never figured out how to do that—especially the *just* part.

Or like being counseled to "*just* say no." I think back on those days when I was surrounded by drugs and sex and all manner of other offers I would never have dreamed of on my own. *Just* say no? I try to picture it, to say it in my mind. Some person I'm wildly in love with, say, takes me in his arms, and I'm in heaven, but I extricate myself and tell him, "No, thank you." No wonder our youth are messed up if we can think of no more explicit advice than that!

As usual whenever I get to thinking about a problem that seems to have no solution, all sorts of information about it comes plummeting out of nowhere. Actually, I always think it comes from *somewhere*, from God himself, even though I typically have to sort it out and connect it up with everything else on my own.

First off, I go to a chapel service at my university, and the speaker starts giving examples of what she calls her "accidental obedience" to God, which comes not out of trying to be good, but as the result of a habit of honoring God. Honoring God, she said, was something like valuing whatever way you like to spend time with God. For her, it was going for a walk. For me, I decided, it's writing. Or, in summer, picking blackberries. Figure out how you enjoy God and take that seriously, she said. That's what she called honoring him.

Not two hours later I was peer evaluating a colleague's biblical studies course. They were discussing the passage from Exodus about the Ten Commandments, and I got put in a group with some students to talk about whether the instruction to "honor thy father and thy mother" was still applicable today. *Honor*, my colleague told us, means "to make heavy" in Hebrew. We tossed that around. Heavy, like a burden, a serious responsibility, someone said. I mentioned the discussions I had recently had with my sister and a friend about what would happen to our parents when they started to be incapable of living on their own.

"I'm at that age where you have to start worrying about that," I said. I didn't tell the students that I wasn't really worried, though, not like my sister probably was, who had nursed my mom through the last years of her life and knew much about the burden of honoring one's parent. Our dad would never leave Southern California and come to Oklahoma to live, I reasoned in my head. And he is hale and active. At seventy, he still regularly bikes to the beaches, often as far as ten miles away. We weren't going to have to start worrying about honoring him for a while yet.

By this time, I was onto God, so I got on the Internet and put in *honor* and *Hebrew* and *heavy* and started reading whatever Google pulled up. This is one of my favorite ways of exploring a topic.

The first result listed was the Web site of Rabbi Michael Ozair, who led something called the OLAM Mystical Wednesdays and seemed to believe in reincarnation. He was exploring the question of why we choose our parents. That all sounded pretty weird to me, but in my experience God is sort of into weird, so I kept reading. Rabbi Ozair considered the views of various rabbis before him, beginning with one from the seventeenth century, and he came to the conclusion that we need to honor our parents because, in our earliest life, we chose them. In his opinion, "To honor our parents means to acknowledge them as people of tremendous worth in our pilgrimage of life. It demands effort and often requires a tolerance for emotional pain, yet it is the most dignified endeavor of an entire lifetime."

The next Google results had too many Hebrew words in them for me to make much sense of them, but then, at a Rabbi Michael Gold's cheery site called Heartfelt Communications, I read with interest his answer to Frequently Asked Question #3: Must I obey my parents?

We are told in Exodus to *honor*—that is, to provide for—our father and our mother, he writes. Later, in Leviticus, we are commanded to *fear*—or, as he defines it, "to avoid any action which undermines the dignity, authority, and standing of"—our mother and our father. Nowhere in the Jewish scriptures, Rabbi Gold points out, are we commanded to obey or even to love them. And sometimes, he went on, it's just not possible to love and obey a parent. I could imagine such cases.

What seemed to interest him most was the fact that the father is mentioned first in the honor passage but the mother is mentioned first in the fear passage—just the opposite, he says, of what one would expect. The reason for this reversal, he writes, is that "a person has a natural tendency to honor their mother (who cared for them) and fear their father ("wait until daddy gets home!"). So the Torah goes out of its way to teach that fear and honor apply equally to both parents."

Rabbi Gold's answer to this frequently asked question attracted me because in it he links honor with fear, as, in my experience, is usually the case with those two attitudes. Fear, for me, results from being *dis*honored in some way. Dismissed. Demeaned. Or, as I came to call how I felt after being sexually assaulted, de-mouthed, from the German *entmündigt*, a horrifically literal legal term meaning incapable of speaking for oneself as a result of senility or insanity or some other condition of communicative helplessness. My therapist also linked honor and fear in prescribing honor as the antidote to my abiding fears.

Of course, for Rabbi Gold, fearing one's parents is not bad, but simply their due. There are, Rabbi Gold says, "two aspects of the commandment to respect one's parents, one positive and one negative. There is the positive requirement to provide for one's parents['] physical needs. And there is the negative prohibition never to detract from the dignity and standing of a parent." I tried the Rabbi's equation out on myself. Honoring my own needs might mean, in the positive sense, providing for myself and, in the negative sense, not compromising my dignity or standing as an individual.

This seemed to me a good place to leave the modern Jews and return to the old ones. The verses containing the word *honor* that my Bible concordance listed were surprisingly unenthusiastic on the subject of honor—especially seeking it for oneself. The story of Esther, in particular, mentions honor in just about every verse as something that only the bad guys are trying to get. And Proverbs repeatedly denounces it outright: "It is not good to eat too much honey, nor is it honorable to seek one's own honor" (25:27). Honor, it seems, is okay to give but not to receive.

At the breakfast table the next morning, I asked my husband if he thought it was okay to honor one's own needs. He said he thought it was not only okay but that one of what Jesus called the two greatest commandments, to love others as one loved oneself, expressly demanded it. In his view, honor and love amount to the same thing. Before we married, he told me his favorite definition of true love—gleaned from an article in a Phi Beta Kappa newsletter, I later learned—was "esteem enlivened by desire." The two most important commandments, he preached over his poached egg and toast, require us to honor not only God and others but ourselves.

Throughout my life I have feared *and* honored my parents. As a child, I feared my mother's shrieking rages and the threat of my father's much scarier and erratic wrath. My mother promised on countless occasions that my father would punish me when he got home, but I can count on one hand the times he actually did. When he did, though, it was terrifying—the flailing sort of punishment that arises out of frustration and helplessness that I have administered myself in circumstances far less desperate.

My parents loomed in my siblings' and my eyes as monsters of disapproval—particularly our father, who complains nowadays that we make him out to have been an ogre. As children, we feared his size, his loud voice, his sarcasm, his knowledge compared to our own, his disagreement in our Sunday dinner arguments, and even his jokes. Growing up, I never entirely forgave my parents for demanding our instantaneous obedience without explanation or for dismissing our pain as insignificant. I never forgave them for the rage-filled household in which they raised us. Nevertheless, as an adult, I forgive every injustice they ever committed as parents, especially in light of my own struggles as a parent of only two. I also consider their misdeeds the results of even more terrible injustices done to them as children. Thus, I routinely honor them by rendering their suffering heavy.

It may be time, perhaps, my therapist is telling me, that I do the same for myself. It may be time that, instead of fearing the man at the committee meeting or my father or anyone else, I need to fear my own disapproval and self-inflicted punishments, my own jokes. It may be time that I honor myself by recognizing my own hurt and making my own needs heavy—not small and insignificant—in my own eyes.

What are my needs? Like anyone else, like my parents, I need respect, love, forgiveness. I need approval and friendship. I need amusement and a certain predictable sort of safety—of knowing where home is and the pleasant monotony of meals and dishes to wash and my daughters' bedtime rituals. I need my husband and my children. I need to be comforted when I hurt, and I need the special comfort of being the one my children turn to when they are in pain or sad. Even their anger at me when things go wrong tells me they need me. I need that.

Most of all, though, I need what I never realized I had all along: a perfect Parent in addition to my fallible earthly ones. A Father who honors me and loves me, despite my failings, and takes my troubles seriously. A Father entirely worthy of *my* honor. As the chapel speaker said, I need to spend enjoyable time with *that* Father.

So, going on her advice, I sat down at the computer in the upstairs study. When we built the house, it was our plan to call this room the library because a book shelf takes up one entire wall, but then it ended up having two desks and a file cabinet and housing most of the writing and art supplies, so it became the study. My daughters call it the computer room, and every night there is a tussle over who gets to be in there for how long, and every so often someone comes in to root around for paper or glue or scissors or sequins, so it's not the best place for a quiet retreat or for writing.

Having finally managed to oust my older daughter—who was playing Spider Solitaire—and gotten into the flow of the writing, in comes the younger, Lulu, looking for the tape. I made a conscious effort not to sigh.

Lulu is my mean daughter. She is stubborn and imperious and superior acting, very quick to anger, very demanding of others' attention and love, but generally stingy in dispensing it herself. She is also very sensitive about how I respond to her. I'm not allowed to say "Uh-huh" or "That's interesting" or "How nice" in response to anything she tells me, because she regards all of these responses as indications that I'm not truly interested in what she's saying. Likewise, I'm required to establish eye contact whenever she speaks and to close whatever book I might be reading or put down my pencil or cup of coffee. She's all about drop-everything-and-do-my-bidding, and, while I don't want to encourage her in this behavior, I sure didn't want to get her mad right when I was in the middle of writing, so I turned to face her and gravely listened while she told me about her project.

She was making a mixture, she said. Trying not to think about what the bathroom, her usual laboratory for such projects, was going to look like when she got done, I listened, troubleshot about the location of the tape, and, when she eventually found it, went back to my writing.

Two paragraphs later Lulu was back. She had in her hands a plastic sphere from a gumball machine and a snap-together, clear plastic box and held them up for me to see. Inside each glistened a thick, clear liquid studded with colors that caught the light from overhead. The ball glittered in the blue range and the box in the reds and golds. She detailed the ingredients with excitement. They contained water-free soap, some of the perfume she had gotten for Christmas, and two kinds of glitter: the body glitter gels somebody else's parent had thought an appropriate birthday present for a child and then just regular old glitter that I usually hide but that the girls always find—just as they always find the colored sugars we use for iced cookies.

I took the spherical object from her and stared into it as if it were a crystal ball that could tell the future. In it, though, I saw the past. A sweet, searing memory seized me, and I saw a time when glittery things took me as they do my children, when I hoarded a box of shiny objects I'd found in the trash or my mother's dresser or on the street—candy wrappers, loose rhinestones, old tinsel, some pieces of colored glass. I looked up from Lulu's crystal ball and right into her eyes and said, in a moment of clarity or accidental obedience to some unwritten law, "Lulu, I'm honored that you showed me this." And I meant it.

And Lulu, to my astonishment, did a rare thing. Very seriously, as if it were the most important thing on earth, she told me she loved me. Out of the glittery blue. And then she left.

Relevant and cited scriptural passages: Deuteronomy 5:16, Esther 25:26–28, and Matthew 22:34–40.

Other references:

Michael Gold. *Heartfelt Communications.* http://www.heartfelt.com.

Jean Hagstrum. "'Esteem Enlivened by Desire': The Ideal Friendship between Men and Women in Western Culture." *The Key Reporter.* Spring 1984. (In his title, Hagstrum is quoting from a poem called "Spring" by James Thomson (1700–1748).)

Jan Johnson. "Living a Purpose-Full Life." Staley Spiritual Awareness lectures. John Brown University. 19–21 February 2002.

Michael Ozair. *Why We Choose Our Parents.* http://ezinearticles.com.

25

In Memory of Him

O nce a month my church celebrates communion. Since it is a non-denominational church, or perhaps because it is more emphatically Protestant than other churches I have attended since becoming a Christian, our pastor is always careful to point out that the French roll and grape juice we share only *symbolize* Jesus' body and blood. And perhaps, as the only former Catholic there, I'm the only one who notices that transubstantiation is thus consciously ruled out, that the eating of our Savior's body and the drinking of his blood is merely a metaphor, and not the real thing. And of course I agree.

Communion Sunday is my daughters' favorite Sunday of the month, even though the service is almost twice as long, and they loathe a long service. When they were little, they typically peppered even the most riveting sermon with long sighs and overloud whispers: "When is he going to be done?" But on Communion Sunday they persevered stoically, all for the sake of a pinch of bread and a tablespoon of grape juice. They wrenched off shamefully large chunks of bread and, when the metal tray of little plastic cups came their way, they took their time selecting the ones that contained the most juice. They waited excitedly during the pastor's prayer for the moment when they were allowed to raise their piece of Jesus' body to their mouths and then tip the tiny flute of his blood. They licked inside the cup to get the last drop.

As soon as they consumed their portion, they grabbed at my husband and me for our empty cups and secreted them in their pockets for their dolls and stuffed animals to use at tea parties. Once I even caught them wheedling the people in front of us out of their cups. Later in the week, I always found purple smears and dribbles around the hips of their Sunday dresses.

At first I thought that the attraction was those plastic cups, so fragile and captivating, like actual wine glasses in miniature. But the girls seemed to enjoy communion just as much when we cele-brated it differently. Sometimes, instead of passing around the little cups, we would tent one big wine glass of juice and the French roll under a cloth napkin on an artificial wood folding table at the front of our rather pathetic sanctuary in those days—a storefront room dimmed by semitransparent curtains in a derelict strip mall that used to house Wal-Mart before the existing Super Center was built. (My husband liked to tell people back then that we attended church at the old Wal-Mart.)

When it was time for communion, the congregants filed up to the front in family groups while someone played a soft hymn from earlier in the service on the electric keyboard. We were usually one of the first families to approach the table—otherwise we'd have been the loudest family still praying and waiting. The girls pounced on the roll and juice with such alarming zeal that I was always sure they'd end up knocking the glass over and spoiling communion for everyone else.

Lulu, exercising that time-honored right of youngest children, always got to go first. I'd have to wrest the roll from her hands to keep her from claiming most of it. Finally, with great solemnity, she dunked her morsel deep into the glass, then ferried the dripping bread over her cupped hand to her mouth, licking the dribble on her chin with a great flourish.

My daughters have always loved dipping things. I guess all kids do. Even now that they're older, I have to serve them little bowls of seasoned rice vinegar for most potato dishes and salad vegetables, ketchup for brown beans (which they dipped bean by bean as babies), and barbecue sauce for roasted meats.

Until recently, whenever I baked bread and it came fragrant and crusty from the oven, they always demanded grape juice to go with it. They liked to eat the two together, ripping off long pieces of crust and dipping them into the juice over and over again, and when the juice was full of swollen crumbs, they poured it out and got more. They only used certain glasses for this purpose, faceted ones that are small at the bottom and flare out at the top, rather like the little plastic communion cups, but bigger. So, it's a matter of ritual, not mere taste, that governs their communion frenzy, I think. A set of habitual gestures, learned and practiced and revered. Without even truly understanding why, they liked the familiar *process* of communion, and they liked that the bread and juice went together.

I've always wondered why they do go together. Why did Jesus offer us his body *and* his blood, as though his blood were not necessarily to be understood as part of his body? Why didn't Jesus just offer up his body and leave it at that? I would consider my own body incomplete—indeed, meaningless—without my blood pulsing through my veins. Like a movie vampire's victim, my bloodless self would be vacant-eyed, colorless, without hope or even uncertainty, and single-minded the way the girl vampires always are: dream-walking in straight lines, not hearing what anyone is saying to them, staring at other people's throats, always on the verge of inclining the head to lean in and bite and drink. Unreal. Bloodless, my body would be dead, empty, void of the very me-ness of me.

And what, for that matter, is the meaning of our Judeo-Christian preoccupation with blood to begin with? When I first became a Christian, my husband and I attended a Baptist church. Everything was new to me then. The tiny town in eastern Oklahoma where we lived was more foreign than Berlin, Beijing, or Hong Kong—the places I had been living. People not only talked and dressed differently than I did, they fought and loved and even prayed differently. My mother-in-law got offended because I didn't wave at her house as I passed by at six-thirty in the morning on my way to work. Elderly neighbors I had never met seemed to expect me to recognize their voices on the phone. Faculty at a school assembly got upset when I pronounced the word *penalize* with the long *e*, which someone later explained to me wasn't the way they pronounced that word and reminded them of the word *penis*, a word one must never mention in Oklahoma or even inadvertently call to others' minds.

Local Christians were especially perplexing. I had colleagues who had never cut their hair their whole lives and students who were not allowed to attend dances and friends who were outraged at the slightest obscenity in a movie but watched the smuttiest stuff you could imagine on TV all the time.

The Christian living in my own house baffled me most. Even before I became a Christian and we both started attending church, my husband insisted on our tithing ten percent of every penny we earned. And so we sent out regular checks to the Salvation Army, a food charity called Hope, Habitat for Humanity, the Sierra Club, Amnesty International, and Greenpeace (until they abandoned environmental activism in favor of global politics, in our estimation). I routinely came upon my husband on his knees in our walk-in closet, praying. Only after I had been reading the Bible for a number of years did I learn that he did this because he had taken to heart a King James directive from his youth: "But thou, when thou prayest, enter into thy closet, and when thou hast shut thy door, pray to thy Father which is in secret; and thy Father which seeth in secret shall reward thee openly" (Matthew 6:6).

I kept trying to figure out how things worked, standardizing them in my mind so that I could predict what might be expected of me when the time came. The local church services were the very worst. Having long since abandoned the Catholicism of my youth, I yet yearned for its rituals, tidily laid out for newcomers in the missal stowed behind each pew. When to kneel and when to stand. When to speak and what to say. When to pray. When to make little cross signs on my forehead, lips, and chest. In the masses of my childhood, just before communion, the priest held up the bread and the chalice of wine, saying, "Let us proclaim the mystery of faith," and we responded on cue: "Christ has died; Christ is risen; Christ will come again." I liked knowing what the mass was all about.

I could never tell what these Baptists were up to, though. Their services seemed formless. There was no missal, no discernable order of events besides a bulletin that listed who was sick or had died or was getting baptized. Congregants were always getting up during the service and walking around—sometimes in groups to kneel at the front, other times to reel singly down the center aisle to be met mid-sanctuary by the preacher. Even their songs were impossible, with rollicking, unpredictable melodies and too many words, and all of the songs seemed to be about either the sea or blood or sometimes both. Washing in blood. Purchased with blood. Redeemed by the blood. Blood-washed throngs. Precious blood. Power in the blood. Fountains filled with blood.

The way I see it, crucifixion was a relatively blood-free death, as violent deaths go. Jesus probably did bleed some. The Messiah had to bleed and be pierced to fulfill scripture. He bled from the crown of thorns and the nails pounded into his hands and feet, and we know that he sweated blood in the Garden of Gethsemane and that blood and water flowed from his dead body when soldiers pierced it with a spear to make sure he was dead. But crucifixion kills by slow suffocation, medical experts say. The bloodiness of Jesus' death would have been incidental—and minor compared to John's or anyone else's beheading—and it certainly would have been less bloody than if he had been stabbed to death or shot full of arrows or eviscerated or drawn and quartered or eaten by lions or killed by most of the methods used to kill Christians in the gory *Little Pictorial Lives of Saints* that I loved to read as a child.

Instead, Jesus died a virtually bloodless, less dramatic, humbler death. He was one of three people, common criminals, executed in exactly the same way. There was little actual violence to watch, merely the humiliation of being laughed at in his misery and having placards hung on him and being displayed naked up in the air for all below to look up at. It takes a long time for someone who has been crucified to die, so many of those watching probably left the scene while Jesus was still alive. When the soldiers came back later to hasten the three criminals' death by breaking their legs so they could no longer hold themselves up and keep their ribcages extended enough to breathe, they found Jesus already dead. No one in authority had even noticed. They stabbed his side almost as an afterthought, an idle desire to see if it was true, as they thought at the time, that the blood and the water would separate if the body was dead. In the case of Jesus' dead body, they apparently did.

My childhood Catholic church pretty much left the blood out of the communion service—at least for us parishioners. Far away at the front of the church, behind the massive altar, the priest did swish together some wine in a chalice with a dribble of water to create—not merely symbolize—the blood and water that flowed from Jesus' pierced side. But only the priest actually drank this mixture. When the rest of us approached the communion rail and knelt, we received nothing but a flat little disk of bread that the priest held up and then placed on our outstretched tongues. Indeed, a little wine—or grape juice, for that matter—would have been a great improvement on the sacrament, in my opinion, because, since we weren't supposed to chew Jesus' body but merely swallow it, it usually adhered itself to the roof of my mouth before I could get it down.

As a freshman in college, I went to church a few times at the student center, where we all—even the priest, who wore regular clothes—sat on the carpet in a circle to celebrate mass. When it was time for the Eucharist, we passed around a plastic champagne glass—the kind with the detachable stem they have at weddings— full of Gallo Hearty Burgundy. I remember the brand because it was my dad's wine of choice and I had noticed a mostly empty half-gallon bottle of it under the folding table on which the communion items, as at my church now, were displayed. I remember feeling adult to be drinking wine, and I worried about spilling it all over myself trying to pass the hard-to-balance glass to the artsy looking guy—a senior, I guessed—kneeling next to me.

Why was the wine left out of those childhood masses? Why was it added back in when I, and the Catholic church, grew up and got cool? Why doesn't my conservative church, overtly enough against alcohol to translate the wine of scripture as grape juice, just leave out the offending liquid altogether?

The problem of Jesus' blood—what Catholics would appropriately call a mystery—is that it means everything. Not merely the blood covering Jesus when he suffered at our hands, but the gorier blood of our uncleanness—our urges and our hatreds, our humanness—that Jesus assumed when he died for us. It is the blood of our sin as well as the blood sprinkled to cleanse us of sin. The blood of the Israelites' sacrifices. The blood they smeared on their doorjambs to protect their firstborn children from death when the Lord passed over Egypt.

The blood we drink in celebrating communion represents the very essence of Jesus' dual identity as God and man. From his earthly beginning, even as a fetus deep in Mary's uterus, nurtured by the nutrients from *her* blood, Jesus drew life from his own unique blood, blood mysteriously human and divine simultaneously, special blood that made him the living Son of God and also, incomprehensibly, one of us, the Son of Man.

Communion evokes the bitter wine vinegar offered Jesus on the cross and also the wine we will drink with him in heaven. His death and his resurrection to eternal life. The spilled blood of our guilt and the pulsing blood of our hope. Sin. Sacrifice. Celebration. Blood is at the very core of our faith.

Oddly, although I was taught at an early age the bizarre Catholic principle of transubstantiation—that the host really was the body of our Lord and the priest's wine his actual blood—and my catechism teachers gave strict directives on the appropriate or least inhumane way of eating Jesus' actual flesh, I never really found the process of communion grotesque or even weird. As a child, I never wondered exactly what *part* of Jesus' body I was eating. His hand? A rib? And later, as I became more interested in logic and increasingly critical of mixed metaphors and the various hypocrisies of the adult world, I never mulled over why the communion wine, if it really had turned to blood, did not taste salty and faintly metallic, as I knew blood did. And, certainly, when I celebrate communion nowadays as a generic Protestant, I think not about a piece of a human or even godly flesh or about a little plastic flute of actual blood but about my sin and the amazing love that sees beyond it.

Eating God's body and drinking his blood is simply a medium for reminding myself about redemption. It's just something Christians do. And, to be absolutely honest, when I eat my piece of stale bread and drink my little cup of lukewarm juice, I'm usually preoccupied with my children's possible misbehavior—across the church from us, where they now sit, with people closer to their own ages—and how I might be embarrassed by it and how envious I am of their enthusiasm, even now that they are older, for a crust of bread and a drop of grape juice, for the ritual of it.

I guess this is why I haven't gotten out the Bible and read to my daughters what the apostle Paul says about not taking communion seriously, even though the passages, when I consider them, seem directly relevant to their communion zeal. I never tell them that "the kingdom of God is not a matter of eating and drinking" (Romans 14:17). Or, "whoever eats the bread or drinks the cup of the Lord in an unworthy manner will be guilty of sinning against the body and blood of the Lord" (1 Corinthians 11:27). I don't admonish them: "Anyone who eats and drinks without recognizing the body of the Lord eats and drinks judgment on himself" (1 Corinthians 11:29). I guess I figure that their enthusiasm for the Lord's Supper goes beyond the little glasses and the dipping, that what they like is being a part of things, getting to participate in something fun that is taken seriously by the grownups, and that there is something essential about communion that they understand and I don't. And I envy it.

It is the nature of children to understand nothing and understand everything. They don't ask the questions of our doubt— What is truth? How can a man be born again when he is old? They don't pray the unbeliever's prayer—Lord, help my unbelief. They believe what is obviously true, without question. They aren't bothered by a mixed metaphor. They have genuine, unadulterated, unself-conscious faith. Jesus recognized this in children and recommended that we mimic it.

The other evening I was sick in bed, and Charlotte came in to try to make me feel better. She fancies herself the family nurse, as I used to when I was a child. Even though it isn't Christmas time and she has long since outgrown picture books, she read me *The Polar Express,* which she claimed was her favorite book. I asked her what she liked about it, and she said, unequivocally, "The pictures."

She showed me her favorite picture—of wolves watching the Christmas train from the snowy woods—and then she showed me her favorite wolf, who stood closest to the speeding train, almost out of the woods entirely, in an attitude of yearning. After that she paged chronologically through the book, sometimes reading the printed words, sometimes commenting in her own words or pointing out what was going on in one of the book's truly wonderful illustrations.

"And here is the bell," she said, turning past the story's end to a close-up painting of the first Christmas present, which the boy in the story had had the fortune of getting to choose, then the great misfortune of losing, and finally the even greater fortune of having restored to him on Christmas morning by Santa himself.

"You wouldn't be able to hear it because you're a grown-up," Charlotte reminded me solemnly, "but I could."

Relevant and cited scriptural passages: Matthew 6:6, Luke 22:14–20, Romans 14:17, and 1 Corinthians 11:27–29.
Other references:
George E. Burch and Nicholas P. DePasquale. "Death by Crucifixion." *American Heart Journal.* Volume 66, Issue 3, 1963. (p. 434–5).
William Cowper. "There Is a Fountain Filled with Blood." 1771.
Lewis E. Jones. "There Is Power in the Blood." 1899.
"Memorial Acclamation." The Mass of the Roman Rite.
John Gilmary Shea. *Little Pictorial Lives of Saints.* 1878.
Chris Van Allsburg. *The Polar Express.* 1985.

26

Fantasia on Children,
Critical Thinking, and Sex

The other day one of my colleagues—a professor of business holding a doctorate of law who is a practicing immigration lawyer, a CPA, a novelist, a songwriter, and a proficient player of whatever musical instrument he touches—preached by popular demand in chapel. Don's sermon, based on a close reading of the story of the prodigal son, was, in essence, a call to innocence, to being like a little child just as Adam and Eve were in the garden before their fateful attainment of the knowledge of good and evil. In order to get back to the father, Don argued, the prodigal son had to quit trying to be a grown-up and just be a little child. Don has always liked, he said, Jesus' elevation of children to the status of those greatest in faith.

The sermon was, as it always is when Don preaches, delightfully brazen and thought-provoking and ended in one of his silly and equally thought-provoking songs, called "Rapidly Approaching Zero," in which the singer keeps getting younger and younger in age and closer to zero, a state celebrated in the refrain as "the less of me, the more of Father."

After the service, many of my other colleagues—notably those in the division of biblical studies—were up in arms about the sermon's anti-intellectual message. We're all about "loving God with our minds" at my university, and the general consensus seemed to be that the return to childhood Don was encouraging amounted to an abdication of pursuits of the intellect.

It's funny how often the themes of one of a day's events resonate with events before and after it. I had been pondering a similar conflict for weeks. My church had been struggling through 1 Timothy and finally arrived at that alarming passage where Paul states,

> A woman should learn in quietness and full submission. I do not permit a woman to teach or to have authority over a man; she must be quiet. For Adam was formed first, then Eve. And Adam was not the one deceived; it was the women who was deceived and become a sinner. But women will be saved through childbearing—if they continue in faith, love and holiness with propriety. (2:11–15)

During our church's usual discussion following the service, one of my fellow church members, a professor like me, said of the passage that, if one of his students had written it in a paper, he'd give it a low grade for bad logic and weak thinking. In response, an elder, another professor, became enraged. At first I thought the elder merely took offense at the comparison of the God-breathed Bible to other pieces of writing, but as he fumed it became clear that what so upset him was that the other piece of writing to which the Bible was implicitly compared was not just any writing but "a *student's* writing." He repeated those outraged words several times with that emphasis, meaning: the writing of someone untrained in theology, someone who knew nothing at all about God, a virtual child in the faith.

I had also been working my way through the latest *Atlantic Monthly*, beginning with the letters to the editor, which are always one of my favorite parts. One letter, from an irate physicist, referenced an ongoing—usually *ad hominem*—debate in academia about the scholarly value of the views of scholars writing outside their fields. According to the angry physicist, unless you know everything there is to know on a subject—that is, everything that respected scholars in the field have ever written on the subject—then your opinion is worth diddly-squat.

As these arguments came together in my mind, I was struck by the sameness of the epistemological assumptions underlying them. Professors are smarter than students. The educated are the only ones worth listening to on any subject. Adults are better thinkers than children. Scholarship is a matter of knowing everything about one subject rather than something about many subjects. Renaissance women and men—like Da Vinci, who was an expert in engineering and science and a hundred other fields as well as painting and sculpture—are out. Single-minded specialists in one field are in. Intellectualism is about quantity of knowledge and how long one's been at it rather than the quality of one's thinking.

I've been thinking about these assumptions—outside of my field of knowledge, of course, which is *neither* philosophy nor psychology nor theology—and I have come to the conclusion that my colleague Don is right in seeking to combat them. My students *teach* me far more than they ever learn from me. The educated are often the biggest asses I know, and the ones whom I occasionally have to listen to at conferences who know everything that has ever been written on a single topic are usually the least inspiring. Connecting many subjects is worth far more to me than knowing everything about one subject. And children, in my experience—in addition to having greater faith than adults, if we can trust Jesus as an expert in these matters—are the best thinkers I have ever encountered.

Children have to be smart, for one. In an amazingly short period—a couple of years to be exact—even the dullest of them metamorphose from blobs of flesh capable only of screaming, squirming, sleeping, sucking, and making waste, into complex beings capable of reasoning, of communicating with others, and of making decisions—whether to obey or disobey, to whine or wheedle, to lie or tell the truth. They learn all this through the age-old academic techniques of copying others, daring to try something new, and, above all, questioning.

Children are masters of the question. Even before they can talk, they question in sign language. As a toddler, Lulu would grab up a raw cookie from the baking sheet about to go in the oven, but before stuffing it into her wet mouth, she would look up at me quizzically to make sure it was okay. In Wal-Mart I see babies perform the same action, pointing at a balloon some other child has or a toy on the shelf and then looking back at Mom in a successful communicative act no one ever taught them to perform. And as soon as the child can talk, the questioning never stops. What is a pimple? Why didn't you punish Sister, too? They master intricately ironic rhetorical questions, such as, having just created chaos and devastation in a public place, "Why are we leaving?"

Of course, adults and even some adult scholars ask questions, too, but the nature of the questions is significantly different. Children ask mostly *What* and *Why* questions, whereas more mature thinkers ask in the realm of *Who*, *When*, *Where*, and *How*.

Check this out if you don't believe me. Listen to your church's debates on theological issues and compare them to your children's. When my nephew was just little, my sister Dorothy called and said she had told him the rudiments about God—that he created the animals and plants and the sky and the sun and people and the whole world.

"Why?" he wanted to know, asking a question far more revelatory of the nature of God and his relationship with us than the zillions of questions theologians get mired in about the who, when, where, and how of creation. Even if we knew how long a day was or the location of Mount Ararat or whether God clapped his hands in a big bang or simply blew a swirling wind to start it all, while it might reveal something of his power, it would show us little about his will or his plans for the future and nothing about his love or his longings on our behalf, the characteristics that differentiate him from the gods of most myths and legends.

Children are also not daunted by sticky questions like the ones every Christian I knew sidestepped when I first started reading the Bible. Just like a child—or, in any case, like my children and like I was when I was young—I was drawn to contradictory information. *Why can't believers lose their faith?* I wanted to know. *Why would Jesus change water to wine if drinking alcohol was bad?* (Most of my Christian friends then were teetotaling Baptists.) *Why do we get so much instruction from Jesus on how to be good if none of it is going to merit anything, according to Paul?*

Invariably, those I asked either ignored my question and started pontificating on some other pet topic of their own, or else they got outright mad at me—just as I do at my daughters—for being bellicose and nitpicky and—secretly, I think—for challenging what they held dear. It's those *why* questions, the kind that drive the mature mind nuts, that make thinkers out of screamers and poopers.

Not long ago, on our way home from grocery shopping, my daughters were discussing Anne Frank. We had been to see a play version of the thirteen-year-old's diary weeks before, and in the back seat of the car my daughters were debating the touchy question of whether the girl, a mere child not much older than they were, had gone to heaven.

Both girls recalled every detail of her merciless death reported at the end of the play. In her father's last glimpse of her, shortly before she died of typhus at Bergen-Belsen and only days before the prisoners of the concentration camp were finally freed, she clung to the barbed wire surrounding the camp, almost naked, her head shaved because of lice, crying.

"I'm all alone," she told her father. Her mother and sister had both already been murdered.

"Do you think she went to heaven?" Lulu asked her older sister.

Charlotte considered. "She was nice to everyone. And in the play she said she thought people were good."

"But she didn't believe in God," Lulu said.

I couldn't help interjecting from the driver's seat that actually the Jews did believe in God, the very same God as the one we worship as Christians.

"But she didn't believe in Jesus, did she?" Lulu insisted. "So she went to hell."

But Charlotte strained against the truth she too had been taught.

"It would be too mean. Too sad. I don't believe God would let that happen. It's just too sad."

Up in the front seat, I drove, staring heavily at the car in front of me to keep from crying, because it always makes the girls mad when

216

I cry. The theological question they explored, while commonplace enough, was more heartfelt, truer somehow, than if they were adults arguing it from some sawed off stump of mature opinion. Children think unabashedly with their hearts, just as Jesus was always trying to get the Pharisees to do. Meanness, although children practice it themselves, just doesn't make sense to them in a loving God, so they reject it.

Children, unlike adults, are also profoundly concrete. This attention to sensual details is evident in their writing and their art. While I have to show my college students how to be concrete in their writing—and even after showing them how I have to remind them again and again to do it—children do it naturally. Ask them to defend a view—like that smoking's bad—and they will automatically begin describing what they have witnessed themselves: yellowed teeth and fingers, how a friend whose mother smokes smells bad, how funny it looks when people suck in a lungful. Only then will they offer the details that they have been taught about the cancer it causes or the tar that builds up in a smoker's lungs or how expensive cigarettes are. Children are in the world. They use their eyes to see, ears to hear, and mouths and fingers and noses to do everything else.

It is because of their observing skills that the artwork of young kids is often so powerful. Young children draw exactly what they see, and their pictures are more accurate, give or take a little for motor skills, than those of more experienced artists. As art professor Betty Edwards argues in her still best-selling drawing textbook of the seventies, *Drawing on the Right Side of the Brain*, to draw more accurately from life, we need to see the world as young children see it. The older children get, the more stylized their art becomes, the less true to life. The eyes they draw become symmetrical and reliably almond shaped, and the eyelashes, all but ignored when they were young, become long and regular and artificial looking. The older they get, the more rigid they become and the less capable of truly discovering truth. Instead of seeing what's before them, they begin to see only what they believe they ought to see. Instead of thinking, they become repositories of knowledge, the used thoughts of others long forgotten.

The smartest people I know of are Supreme Court judges. Nina Totenberg of National Public Radio often reports on new Supreme Court developments by reading transcripts of the justices attempting to find solutions to sticky issues. Virtually everything they say begins with a *What if?* or a *Why then?* or a *Yes but.* Except when my daughters get into it over some matter of importance to one of them, I have never heard such zeal.

Of course, the justices have to inform themselves on the issues and find out what everyone else says is true, but no case is ever a matter of simply finding an expert who knows the right solution and accepting it. No, they have to fight it out. And they fight like children, their ideas as wildly imaginative and their arguments as stodgily logical as only children's claims can be. The problem at issue swells into three, four, five dimensions in their minds, developing fluctuating contours and the lilting rhythms of supposition. It sounds like one big, rowdy play group when I listen to them, and I think, if there were a job I might rather do for money than what I already do—that is, teach people to write—it would be theirs. If, that is, I could only be as smart as a three- or four-year-old.

Here's what makes children so smart. They don't know as much as adults do, so what they know doesn't get in the way of actually thinking. They think with relentless precision, with the bold logic of *why*, unfettered by self-doubt, never afraid to ask the key question of the true intellectual: What does that mean?

I give my students extra credit for daring to ask what they think of as stupid questions: *What does that mean? Why do we look at it that way? Why can't we see it this other way? What does this have to do with that?* These, for me, are the only truly intelligent questions. All other questions are about power and control and status, not about thinking but about already knowing. They're not really questions at all. Smart questions, on the other hand, are questions that genuinely seek answers.

Children's method of inquiry is more truly scientific than that of most scholars whose work I read. Children are naturally inductive in their thinking. They begin by observing, then they probe and test, then observe some more before they ever come to any conclusion. They tend to skip hypothesis altogether, jumping from observation right on into the extraordinary claims modern science says should never be made without extraordinary evidence—and for the precise reason that, being new to the world, they find *everything* in it extraordinary, which of course it is.

For this reason, they delight in repetition. "Do it again!" they tell the world around them and then watch, enthralled, for the forty-second time what the adult never found enthralling to begin with. My children have watched the videos they love hundreds of times. When Lulu gets out my husband's old microscope, you have to bribe her to let you have a peep through the eyepiece, even though she's been looking at the same hydras and paramecia for hours.

And, finally, children are experts at learning. Contrary to what education experts will tell you, no child is a visual or auditory or kinesthetic learner or even a combination of the three. They learn with their tongues and their pinky fingers and their imaginations and dreams. They learn with their whole bodies.

Once, when they were little, I overheard my daughters reading aloud, with great hilarity, a description of the sex act from Charlotte's pocket encyclopedia. They found especially funny and revolting how the penis filled up with blood in order to become hard enough to enter the vagina. Charlotte read that part again and again, while Lulu tried to grab the little book out of her hand to look more closely at what I assumed was a picture of the process.

"Let me see!" she whined, "I want to see." They marveled that the details were essentially the same for humans as for dogs and horses, Charlotte's and Lulu's favorite animals respectively, and I could tell from their voices that they were somehow proud of this similarity.

Several times since then, though, my daughters have separately questioned me about the necessity of sexual intercourse and other aspects of reproduction, and they're already worried about Eve's curse, the pain of childbirth.

"I want a baby to *belong* to me someday," Charlotte told me, "but I don't want to *have* it." Lulu plans to become a jockey or a veterinarian, which, in her child logic that I'm too old to figure out, amounts to an renunciation of human sexuality altogether. I have been at pains to explain to either one of them how anyone could ever want to have sex to in the first place.

One afternoon not long afterwards, when I was driving Charlotte to soccer practice, she asked me a litany of questions about the sex act, each one more specific than the last. She was especially interested in the technicalities of arousal. I explicated, with as much precision and as little embarrassment as I could muster, the connection between love and desire, improvising as I went.

"But what does it *feel* like?" she persisted, obviously not satisfied with my perhaps too lapidary description.

I was at a loss.

"I mean," she went on, "is it like when you wake up in the night from a dream about people with no clothes on and you have this feeling that's kind of like you have to go to the bathroom even though you don't?"

I said yes, not allowing myself to feel alarm or even the slightest degree of intellectual approval. But Charlotte wasn't paying any attention to what her mother was feeling or not feeling at that moment.

"I've felt that," she told me, with discernible satisfaction. She had it figured out for now. Like a justice of the Supreme Court, she had looked at sex from all angles. She had thought it through. She had seen a picture of it, consulted the experts, felt it. And, with about the same degree of certainty, the same sense of rightness and enthusiasm that I generally feel when I pencil my comments and the grade at the bottom of a student's paper, Charlotte cast her decision in favor of procreation and everything good and bad that went with it.

Jesus' best friend John, over fifty years after he saw Jesus crucified and resurrected with his own eyes, goes out of his way to reassure believers like me and you, who *didn't* get to meet the son of God in the flesh and have to rely on the Bible for evidence of his existence, that the unschooled faith of our first acceptance of the gospel is all the education in theology that we need: "As for you, the anointing you received from him remains in you, and you do not need anyone to teach you" (1 John 2:27).

John, by the time he wrote those words, was old, probably in the last years of his own life, but he was still hard at work among his squabbling flocks. He refers to them as his "dear children" and to all of us believers as "children of God" to whom "what we will be has not yet been made known" (1 John 3:2). Unlike Paul, John seems to think that remaining as a child is a good thing, an essential anointing that is all we need to understand what we need to know of the Father. Over and over again in John's writings, he celebrates our lofty status as "children of God." And that, finally, is the crux of true theology: to recognize and enjoy just "how great is the love that the Father has lavished on us, that we should be called children of God! And that is what we are!" (1 John 3:1).

Relevant and cited scriptural passages: Matthew 18, Mark 10, John 1:12 and 11:52, I Timothy 2:11–15, and I John, (especially 2:27 and 3:1–2).

Other references:

Frances Goodrich and Albert Hackett. *The Diary of Anne Frank.* 1956.

Don Balla. Chapel presentation. John Brown University. 9 April 2002.

Don Balla. "Rapidly Approaching Zero." *Rapidly Approaching Zero* 1999.

Betty Edwards. *Drawing on the Right Side of the Brain.* Los Angeles: Tarcher, 1979.

John Frandon. *D K Pockets Encyclopedia.* Dorling Kindersley, 1997.

27

Love and Fairness

Every morning my husband gets up a half hour before me—at 5:00 a.m.—to shower and fix our coffee. He either listens to and interprets the noises I try not to make upstairs so as not to wake the children or else he follows some internal clock that can predict how long it will take me that day to bathe and figure out what I'm going to wear and locate the book I'm currently reading. In either case, as soon as I slump into my blue chair at the kitchen table, he slides my oversized cup of coffee and frothed milk in front of me. This is one of my daily blessings. I don't ever tell Kris so, and often, in my morning gruffness, I don't even thank him. I don't say much at all that early in the morning. And even though his morning duties are matched by my afternoon ones—washing our clothes and cooking our supper—I always feel that I don't merit such extraordinary gifts as my morning coffee and this man who rises in the dark and brews and froths and measures the sounds of my waking.

I also don't deserve his other little tricks of kindness—how, after breakfast, he fills my water bottle and puts on my clogs to carry it and my book bag out to the car. Outside he sings his morning greeting to our dogs and gives them their breakfast. In the winter, he even starts the car for me and lets it idle there to defrost the windows and heat up. He sets it at 79°. I've always wondered how he came to that temperature. Why not 78° or 80°? It is one of the mysteries I ponder as I drive to work. How came it that I married him? That we are so blessed with healthy daughters and a house to live in? Is it right for me to enjoy such luxuries as frothed milk and heated vehicles?—not merely in light of such considerations as world poverty and the pollution to which that extra ten minutes of gas contributes, but in real terms, eternal terms. What does it mean that we thrive, while others suffer?

Usually I listen to the news on my way to work, and the contrast between my life and the lives of others—victims of earthquakes and wars and hideous diseases and workplace shootings—worries me. It cannot be that I am *particularly* loved by God, I muse. I am not more loving or charitable or pious than others.

And so a wickedness of worry wells up in my soul, the certain knowledge that my time is coming. Before long—and indeed, when it happens, these happy days of morning coffee and warm cars will belong to a past immeasurably distant—before long, I worry, one of my daughters will die or our house will burn down or cancer will make it impossible for me digest my food or even desire a cup of coffee. I struggle almost daily against the heresy that everything evens out, that God is—as my daughters and my students and every pedagogical resource I've ever read want *me* to be—inexorably fair. Good parents and teachers never discipline in anger or favor one child or student over another. If God truly is the perfect parent, the perfect teacher, I reason uneasily, surely he establishes clear boundaries for us all and metes out clearly-stated consequences for breaching them, punishing and rewarding us just as equally, the same for everyone.

Even now, as I write, I doubt what I know to be true. Are these worries really heretical? Isn't God just? Isn't that what justice means: that nobody gets a better shake than anyone else?

I think, in our culture, we've come to view justice that way. We speak of our inalienable rights, justice and liberty for all, and we feel entitled to what we've earned. We expect our governing bodies and fellow citizens to provide for our needs. And when we are denied our rights or disenfranchised or not taken care of, we call it injustice.

But the just God I keep coming up against is one who seems frivolous and disturbingly selective in his provision, showering me with blessings I *haven't* earned, providing for me so generously that I'm not even conscious of any unmet needs, while all around me are pains and sorrows I can hardly fathom.

The scriptures offer example after example of God's wrathful discipline, too: the flood, Sodom and Gomorrah, the sudden deaths of Ananias and Sapphira, Moses not getting to enter the promised land. God himself says he's slow to anger, not that he doesn't get angry at all, and it seems that he comes down harder on some sinners than he does on others, even others who commit the very same sins.

Also, embarrassing as this is to admit, his boundaries aren't all that clearly drawn to me. It's not entirely clear to me what all the rules are that I should be following, what with the old law—its degrees of sin ranging from murder to mildew—versus the one written on my heart. (Imagine explaining that violation to a fractious seventh grader: "You know, you broke one of those rules written on your heart!") Neatly put, God's not fair.

And so, I believe I'm wrong to expect disasters, which isn't to say they won't happen. But if they do, they won't be payback, but rather—I try to believe this—new opportunities for God to show his very particular love for me.

This morning we were in a hurry, and it wasn't cold enough for there to be frost, so my husband didn't start my car before I left. After the flurry of finding the girls' coats and pouring Kris's tea for work and locating all the things I needed to put in the car and then rushing back to the house to get my bottle of water, I finally put my key in the ignition and was on my way. I was halfway down our road before I thought to turn on the heater, and when I did, it came on to exactly 79°, as always. Only then did I realize that the temperature is preset in our car to come on at the temperature it was last on. Although Kris must have selected that temperature sometime in the past, it was not someone's specific and moment-to-moment loving forethought that determined my blessings, but—as my non-Christian friends are always trying to persuade me is the case with God's blessings—an array of events set in motion by habit and nature and, in this case, the car's electronic memory. Strangely, though, learning this has not made me think Kris's—or God's—love for me any less strong but rather confirms a basic tenet of faith that my daughters have been teaching me from babyhood: God cannot be mean. Meanness is simply not in his character.

God, in my daughters' view, wants to give us good things, which is their defense of praying for the toys and events they yearn for, and he deeply desires his children's happiness. For this reason, he made Kris and me Charlotte's and Lulu's personal servants. And he made dogs and cattle and the forests and fields that surround our house. He made the persimmon trees and loaded them with the sugary fruit that Charlotte and Lulu gather after the first hard frost. And the thrilling "ravine," as they call a dry ditch that bisects a far field littered with cow skeletons. And the rain that fills a depression beside our gravel driveway and makes a cool muddy puddle for the dogs. As toddlers, after a summer rain, Charlotte and Lulu peeled off every shred of clothing to roll in that puddle with the dogs. And to this day, though they have long outgrown stripping to their bare, glorious skin and playing in the mud, they remain reverent toward the puddle. Last year, when I wanted to fill in the depression with rocks excavated from my gardening, they forbade it.

My daughters, as little ones, were such staunch believers in God as the provider of all good things that they became amazed, outraged, when something went awry—when their puppy broke its leg or one of their dairy calves got screw worms. They never fully learned one important spiritual lesson of disaster—that humans are usually the ones behind it—but their fervent prayers in response to these tragedies have taught me another truth they earnestly believed in: God fixes things. What we mess up, he longs to fix.

The question of whether or not God is fair, however, stumps even Charlotte and Lulu, as it has stumped believers over the centuries, and I anticipate it will consume them more and more as they encounter the blessings and apparent miseries that lie before them. The ultimate misery, of course, is death, and the ultimate blessing, surviving it. It won't be long, I expect, before my daughters are asking me questions relevant to these eventualities—the questions of my faithless friends, the questions of my own past as a nonbeliever, the questions I still sometimes ponder when I consider the miracle of my salvation.

"How is it that only those who know Jesus are saved?" people critical of Christianity always want to know. "What about Muslims?

What about Jews? And what about those who have never even heard of Jesus? Or those who die as babies? Or before they were even born?"

The believers who stand in their midst may not have any answers. They may, in fact, struggle themselves with related faith questions involving the availability of faith and the degree of responsibility we have in pursuing it. I know a lot of Christians who do.

"What about those who are born without brains with which to recognize Jesus if they could see him, much less understand the words of the gospel?" a man I go to church with once asked. He has a disabled grandson and has spent a lot of time in hospitals, and he tells painful stories of those worse off than his grandson, people who live at the hospital and are never visited and wouldn't know it if they were. "What about nonbelievers in comas? Or the severely mentally ill, who perhaps unwittingly deny God or even seek their own deaths? What about the demon possessed, if there is such a thing as demon possession? In scripture, the ones who have demons don't seem to have much control over their circumstances and often have to rely on other people to bring them to Jesus' notice. Where's the justice in that?"

It seems to me that whole denominations of believers have developed from the attempt to resolve the question of divine justice. A Methodist friend of mine worships a democratic God, who proffers eternal life equally to all of his children, whether they want it or not. Some of my Calvinist friends worship a wily-sounding and selective God, who picks out in advance the ones he wants to favor with eternal life and, by extension, the ones who will go to hell. In the Catholic faith of my youth, I worshipped God the Rewarder, who granted eternal life to the well behaved and relegated those who died without being baptized, such as stillborn babies and very sick or unconscious people with unconfessed minor sins, to limbo, a handy holding place from whence—my childhood catechism teacher tried to reassure us—it might still be possible for them to be saved some day from eternal damnation.

Each solution to the problem of divine justice second guesses God, it seems to me. But I suppose they're no worse than my own concept, that I struggle to suppress, that someday I will get my comeuppance for a husband who makes my coffee in the morning and a virtually trouble-free existence. In these worries, I worship a fair but rather mean-spirited God, one who evens things out and will eventually send tragedies to even out our blessings.

Today, though, I choose to worship a God whose justice is beyond my understanding in all particulars but this one that my children have taught me: God is not mean.

God gave me a husband who loves me and children who are not horribly sick and a job I like and a mother-in-law who passes on her cars to us for their bluebook prices and, two Sundays ago, eight newborn Labrador puppies who are just now opening their eyes. (There were nine, actually, but the runt died in the night, and the girls said it was a good thing because their mom, Tessi, only has eight nipples.) God hears my prayers and answers them in my best interest, every one of them, although I sometimes don't recognize that he has or agree with him about what my best interest might be.

And as for those Old Testament faithful who lived before Jesus and didn't get a chance to actually meet him, in Hebrews 11 we learn that God has prepared a city for them, too, for, while "they did not receive the things promised"—such as coming of the Messiah —they nevertheless "saw them and welcomed them from a distance" (11:13). They, in other words, longed for God's promises to be fulfilled, and in response to that longing, God has prepared for them, as for all of his other children of faith, a place with him in heaven.

And if we deem merely longing for God too specific and onerous a task to be a fair requirement for receiving eternal life, consider how those faithful ones expressed this longing. According to the writer of Hebrews, all they did was admit "that they were aliens and strangers on earth" and thereby "show that they are looking for a country of their own [. . .] a better country—a heavenly one" (11:13, 14, 16). They longed to be somewhere else. Somewhere better. It seems to me that even sick newborns, even those without brains to think with and the mentally ill and those possessed of demons, indeed all those who suffer the wretchedness of being significantly ill equipped for this world, must yearn for heaven daily.

"Blessed are the poor in spirit," Jesus begins a long list of promises, "for theirs is the kingdom of heaven" (Matthew 5:3). That's the God I'm worshipping today, a God incapable of heartlessness.

I am already having to reassure my daughters on this point, although I learned it from them to begin with.

"You're right," I tell them when I overhear them debating Anne Frank's salvation or what happens to aborted babies. "God *isn't* mean. He doesn't abandon those who seek him. And he takes care of all those who suffer. After all, he made us. Without him, we wouldn't even exist."

This is a thought that has always sobered Charlotte and Lulu. They can't comprehend such a dreadful state as nonexistence. When they were little, they got mad if I even mentioned it. Back then, they liked to think they had always existed, even before they were born, before they were ever conceived, that they lived before their advent on earth just as Jesus did up in heaven with God. One of my theologian friends has told me this belief in the preexistence of souls was a popular heresy, called Apokatastasis, attributed to the early church father Origen of Alexandria in the third century.

I've been reading Augustine's *Confessions* lately and have noticed that he, like my daughters, was tempted by this heresy. "Tell me, God," he writes, "tell your suppliant, in mercy to your poor wretch, tell me whether there was some period of my life, now dead and gone, which preceded my infancy? Or is this period that which I spent in my mother's womb? . . . What was going on before that, my sweetness, my God? Was I anywhere, or any sort of person?" Augustine makes no apology for his speculations, except to comment that God "may smile at me for putting these questions." While his faith on this point, as he explains to God and his readers, "may be limited to that which I know," he clearly values and indulges his own God-given ability to imagine answers to his questions.

Charlotte and Lulu, when they're feeling especially affectionate, occasionally play a game with me they made up in babyhood in which they list all the reasons why, up in heaven together before their births, they chose me and Kris to be their parents out of all the people in the world. It is a wonderful game full of near disasters— "We almost picked Kaitlyn's mom. She likes indoor dogs. But she's not as good of a cook as you are!"—but in the end Kris and I reign as the best of all possible parents, and the game has a simple underlying message I can't hear enough from my children: we love you.

I have a secret fantasy similar to this heretical childhood game of theirs that I turn to when I botch things up as a parent, or when things aren't going so well with Kris or one of the girls, or when things are great and I am worrying about all the bad things that must necessarily be in the works for me. In my fantasy, God is up in heaven looking down delightedly on all of creation. It must be before the fall or else his x-ray eyesight is somehow obscured—by love or longing, probably—but he sees only the good things about the world. He looks down on us and seizes us up one by one to love on us, each time more enthusiastic than the last—pretty much the way Tessi ferociously licks her puppies each one in turn. I am standing in a crowd of people waiting, most of us looking up enviously, wanting to be next. And finally he gets to me. He looks down at me and recognizes me and sees me for what I am. And still he reaches down his big hand and beams at me in utter enchantment.

God is not mean. He chose me, despite my own frequent meanness. He chose me when there were better people. Better mothers. Better writers. Better Christians. Better cooks, probably. There are so many others that he could have chosen, others that I hope he will choose, every one of them. And after he chose me he has kept on choosing me: rewarding me, reassuring me, burying me in blessings.

Our God, I have learned from my daughters, is the God of promises—promises of healing and happiness and all good things—for those who look forward to their fulfillment. Promises available not only in the Word of God but in all creation, in newborn puppies with their eyes still closed and ditches and frothed milk and silly games. In children. In our ability to imagine heaven.

Relevant and cited scriptural passages: Genesis 6, 7, and 19; Deuteronomy 32:48–52; Exodus 34:5–7; Matthew 5:3; Acts 5; and Hebrews 11:13–16.
Other references:
Augustine. *Confessions.* Henry Chadwick, trans. Oxford: Oxford UP, 1991, (p. 1).
Origen. *De Principiis (Of First Principles).* Circa 231.

Rest

28

The Water Jar

T his morning I was leafing through the Bible looking for a place where someone said we become what we worship. I remembered being much struck by the passage when I had first read it, and I was sure I had written as much in the margin. I didn't find the line I was looking for, but I did notice a *Wow!* scribbled in the margin next to this passage in the gospel of John: "Then, leaving her water jar, the woman went back to the town and said to the people, 'Come, see a man who told me everything I ever did. Could this be the Christ?' They came out of the town and made their way toward him" (4:28–30).

I had to reread the whole story of the Samaritan woman at the well in order to reconstruct my original enthusiasm for these verses. The setting is Samaria, outside the town of Sychar at a place called Jacob's well, probably the nearest source of water to the arid ridge of land Jacob took from the Amorites with his sword and bow and gave to his son Joseph. The time is high noon. I imagine it to be summer or whatever time of year is hot and dry.

Jesus, in any case, is tired and thirsty. He's probably hungry, too.

His disciples, we're told, have left him to go into town to buy food. Having just learned that the Pharisees are becoming concerned about his growing popularity, Jesus and the disciples are on their way through Samaria back home to Galilee. It is a route not typically taken by Jews, and this is one of few scenes in the Gospels where we encounter Jesus utterly alone, sitting down by the well, wanting a cool drink but unable to get one because, as the Samaritan woman will later scoff when he starts talking about giving her living water, he has "nothing to draw with and the well is deep" (4:11). He has to sit and wait for the arrival of some kindhearted stranger with a water jug and something to dip with in order to relieve his thirst.

Jesus is curiously helpless in this cameo from his short life on earth—fleeing unseen enemies, tired, alone, in a place foreign to him, thirsty, and lacking even the most modest means of satisfying his own needs. He doesn't seem aware of the poverty of his circumstances, though, because as soon as the Samaritan woman arrives with her water jar, he starts making big promises. He will give her the gift of God. Living water. A spring welling up to eternal life. She will never thirst again, never again have to trudge to the well in the hot sun with the heavy water jar. He is the promised Messiah, he tells her, who she hopes will come soon and "explain everything."

I've met this sort of man before, I know this woman is thinking. I know I would be. I have met many such: seemingly bereft of all good things—riches, love, loyal friends, even a drink of water— but full of big plans for some far-off golden future.

Our Samaritan woman is imminently practical and sets out to enlighten this stranger about his real situation. He's a Jew, she reminds him, in a strange land, associating with an unclean

Samaritan, and a woman at that. Jesus may be a prophet, she ventures derisively, but—unlike Jacob, whom she refers to as "our father," the revered ancestor of the Samaritans, the people who, she reminds him, worship on the very mountain where they sit talking—he has no land here and no well, no family, no flocks, no herds. She herself at least has a water jar and a dipper and a home to return to. Jesus, she tells him, has nothing.

The story nowhere reveals whether she does or doesn't fetch him the drink of water he requests, but from the woman's hawkish tone I'd guess she doesn't—at least not at first. Get your own water if you're so great, she seems to be arguing.

She continues to belittle Jesus after he orders her to go get her husband and even after she tells him she has no husband and he reveals the details of her own miserable history as a seeker of good things: she's gone through five husbands and now has a live-in lover, someone who hasn't even bothered to marry her for the sake of free sex. To him, she is merely a servant who trudges to the well everyday and makes his meals and washes his clothes. Her water jar about sums up what she has—a way to survive, yes, but at what cost? She prattles on after Jesus' prophetic revelation of her life, but some part of her is struck by his authority and vision, so much so that when Jesus' disciples finally arrive and she runs off to tell the people of the town what has happened, she tells them, "Come, see a man who told me everything I ever did."

Everything she ever did. Was there nothing, no fond memory, no beloved child or prized possession or happy thought, to offset in her mind the misery of what he has shown her of her life? Evidently not. And she leaves immediately to tell the people of the town, people who would have seen her as Jesus did, only without his love: as a drudge and a whore, someone with a water jug but little else. It is amazing to me that anyone even listens to her, much less comes back with her to the well. Why does anyone believe her when she says someone told her everything she ever did? Why do the people she tells even care enough to find out what she means by such a claim? But they do. All I can assume is that they are like her, suffering the same hopeful desolation in this life. Like us all.

And she leaves her water jar behind. This is where I wrote *Wow!* in the margin. Just imagine it. Her very sustenance, worth more than a fortune in a dry land where water sources are so scarce they are given proper names and parched passers-through might sit for hours before a woman kind enough and equipped with a water jar arrives to relieve their distress. And she leaves it behind.

I find this so incredible. Does she forget it in her excitement? Or is it that she knows she'll be coming back to where Jesus is and can retrieve it then? Or perhaps she so thoroughly believes in and trusts his promise, of living water that will quench her thirst for all eternity, that she figures she doesn't need the jug anymore. And what about the earthly thirst that sent her to Jacob's well in the first place, the thirst that she complains requires her to travel out of town at the hottest time of the day to draw? Does that thirst, too, just go away when she meets up with the Christ?

I see in this woman a great gift that I do not have, but one shared by some of the most highly praised of Jesus' disciples. It is the gift of Mary, Lazarus and Martha's sister, who, Jesus tells poor stressed Martha and us, "has chosen what is better, and it will not be taken from her" (Luke 10:42). It is the gift of Peter and Andrew, who abandon their nets, and of James and John, who leave their boats and their father, and of Paul, who embraces imprisonment and death for the sake of the ones he sought to kill.

They have the gift of priorities, the ability to abandon the lesser for the greater, the ability to recognize a pearl of great worth and be willing—no, eager—to give up everything to get it.

"Martha, Martha," Jesus tells her, and us, "you are worried and upset about many things, but only one thing is needed" (Luke 10:41–42).

And what is that? we and the disciples are perpetually asking. It's not a jug, or a net, or a job. It's not an education. It's not your health. It's not a clean record or the great American novel or a lot of good kids who will miss you when you're gone.

"I have food to eat that you know nothing about" (John 4:32), Jesus tells his harried disciples when they arrive at the well with the food. They don't dare question him about the Samaritan woman they find him speaking to. Like her, like me, they are pathetically practical: "Could someone have brought him food?" they whisper among themselves. Who, after all, can survive on nothing more than the will of the one who put us here? That's what Jesus tells them is his food and drink. And they're thinking—you know they are—yes, well, but a person's still got to go out and buy bread.

And so they, and we, like Martha, when faced with a choice, take the hectic, ragged, obvious course we devise for ourselves and abandon God's will to the ones sitting at the Master's feet in the other room. We work like maniacs and build barn after barn to store what we make against the disasters we know are coming. We clutch our water jugs tightly to us, choosing the lesser over the greater, hoping against everything we know to be true that these efforts will afford us at least some sort of measly comfort. And then we suffer in pained silence the resulting chaos.

And Jesus sits on the edge of the well, speaking promises of rest into our frenzied stories, waiting for us to pause a moment, and listen, and breathe.

Relevant and cited scriptural passages: Matthew 4:18–22 and 13:44–46, Luke 10:38–42 and 12:16–21, and John 4:1–42.

29

On Barns

I've never met anyone that didn't like barns. Except maybe my friend Donald, a graphic artist who lives in New York City, who, if I could predict his view of them, would probably group them with milk cans and cider mills as examples of New England kitsch. But everyone else likes a barn. They like its big shape or red color or the muffled air inside or swinging on ropes or memories of hiding from parents and enjoying forbidden pleasures. And, even though most people don't use a barn to store their livelihood in anymore, there is this romantic feeling of serenity about a barn. Of having what one needs against future catastrophes. Of being settled and secure. Of control.

My husband and I got out of farming some years ago to support our family by other means. Reluctantly. Cattle prices had dropped and stayed down, while the price of grain and equipment and other necessities of farming hadn't. My husband went back to school and opened a CPA office in our small town, I took a job teaching English at a nearby university, and our daughters have quit telling the grown-ups who ask that they're going to be cowboys when they grow up but rather teachers or accountants or marine biologists. (We bought a saltwater aquarium after my husband set up his accounting office.)

We still have the farm, a small place by today's farming standards, 380 acres of pasture and woods. We have six barns. In our big hay barn, clad in shiny aluminum, we store square bales left from when we used to have a square baler, as well as most of our remaining hay equipment. A red barn, older and more cheaply built, houses straw. Located in a remote field, it is populated by skunks, so we have to take the shotgun when we go there once a year to get mulch for my mother-in-law's garden. A tall wooden barn about a hundred years old came with the land we bought to build a new house on when we were first married. I couldn't bear to knock it down, as my husband suggested we do for safety reasons, so we invested $6000 in covering it with siding to preserve it. We also use three defunct chicken houses, which once held 15,000 broilers each, to store big round bales in. If we had any use for all this storage space and hay, we'd be all set, but, with most of the land leased out and only a few steers to feed now and then for our own meat, we're barn rich and money poor.

Ironically, barns—even poor old empty ones like ours—symbolize wealth and a lot more. As images, they call to mind the past, the family, this country, certain historical periods and subcultures, the home. They are beautiful structures to many and so frequently the object of paintings as to have become cliché in the artistic context.

An advertisement I saw the other day in a farming magazine we still subscribe to said, "Big Barns Mean Big Profits." Another said, "Bigger barns mean bigger worries, larger dollar losses from fires, bigger liabilities." I know our barns and chicken houses raise our property taxes significantly, even though they are no longer in use. A barn building Web site offers this all encompassing summary: "Barns mean different things to different people."

Think of barns and you think of the Amish—how, without telephones, the neighbors assemble themselves, the requisite tools and building materials, and all those pies. As if barn building needed to respect the three dramatic unities of character, action, and place, the builders are all bearded and wear striking combinations of denim and black, they build the barn in a matter of hours, and then they feast in the open air on slow cooked food and the pies. And, in the photos some outsider takes, the barn looms behind the festivities, the product of their honest hard work and the proof of their eternal security against derision.

This morning I read Jesus' parable about the farmer who keeps getting richer and tearing his barns down to build bigger ones (Luke 12:16–21). He doesn't actually tear down and build the barns in this parable but merely plans to, thinking to himself that if he does, he'll "have plenty of good things laid up for many years . . . Take life easy; eat, drink and be merry." Then God interrupts his scheming, calling him a fool because "This very night" he will die.

Usually, when I read this parable, I think of material things. Money. My husband's fledgling business, thriving but not yet in the black. Buildings we'd like to build. The room we want to add onto our house someday. The carport my husband and I feel we need to protect our car from the elements. And then a new car to replace the elderly used one we bought cheap from his mom when she last bought a new one. We just found out our air conditioning tubing is about to go, and the car is so old it uses Freon gas, which can't be bought for any money, so we'll probably have to buy a new air conditioner. Or go without.

This time, though, after smugly reflecting that I don't really think too much about money or dwell on my family's material needs—which is true; I'm pretty relaxed about financial matters— I got to thinking about the fact that this rich guy hadn't even carried out his plans yet when God told him he was about to die that very night. He was just *thinking* about it. And it occurred to me, suddenly, that this parable was not about storing wealth but about making plans and to-do lists, about living in the future tense instead of now.

My life is one big barely crossed out to-do list. I plan to write more and, more importantly, publish more, perhaps go back to school some more, get more degrees, and teach each class better the next time. I plan to wash the windows some time this year. I plan to plant trees and build a stone wall in front of the propane tank outside the kitchen window where I eat breakfast every morning.

My barns, I got to thinking, are unpublished books, further academic degrees, things to write in future resumes or pleas for salary increases, courses yet to come, a clean house, a pretty yard, a place to rest. And my sin is not these things, many of which I already enjoy, but *thinking* about them—my secret yearning for more job security and professional acclaim and some sort of future leisure in which to garden, read novels, and throw big dinner parties.

I have thought the rich guy's very thoughts: *This is what I'll do. I will tear down my barns and build bigger ones, and there I will store all my grain and my goods. And I'll say to myself, "You have plenty of good things laid up for many years. Take life easy; eat, drink and be merry."* I work long hours, pour my energy and enthusiasm into my students and writing, and then snap at my husband and children when I get home and dream about a future in which this isn't so.

Today I wish to consider the barns I am tearing down: my marriage, my two children, my faith in God to take care of my wants and desires. Jesus begins his parable with a strange statement. He says, "The ground of a certain rich man produced a good crop." The story is about this certain rich man, his schemes and impending death, but the subject of the opening sentence is not the man but the ground—the land, the earth, the very dirt out of which the man himself was made.

Imagine this. God makes a substance so wonderful that it can daily, hourly, recreate itself in endlessly new formats—a branch, a leaf, a fruit, animals, a man and a woman. He sets things up such that the earth continuously supplies its creatures with sustenance— no, with more, with abundance—and ever-changing delight. Its creatures are all rich. Then this earth swells up into a voice that reasons, "I will stop it, store it, keep it, and be even richer some day."

Once, when my daughters were just little, they were discussing verb tenses at the dinner table. We were wanting to make up a story about someone called Eleanor the Onion Eater. I had asked them if it should be about a girl in history or one from now.

"What is history?" Lulu wanted to know. "Is it that backwards time or the one we don't know yet?"

Charlotte haughtily explained that the backwards time was called the past and the time we don't know yet is called the future.

I have been thinking about those definitions, especially that the future is *not* what hasn't yet happened but *what isn't yet known*— and, if I understand Jesus' parable right, what we shouldn't presume to know. My children seem content with this, that there is a time we don't yet know about. As always, my children's way of seeing things is far superior to my own. Planning to build bigger barns is cherishing a future of our own creation rather than the good barns full of what we've already been given. When we plan our futures, we spit on God's gifts and the heaven he has built for us. And in doing so, we create hell.

Relevant and cited scriptural passages: Ecclesiastes 2 and Luke 12:16–21.
Other references:
Aristotle. *Poetics*. 350 BCE.

30

Letting the Master Sleep

My heart is not proud, O LORD,
my eyes are not haughty;
I do notconcern myself with great matters
or things too wonderful for me.
But I have stilled and quieted my soul;
like a weaned child with its mother,
like a weaned child is my soul within me.
O Israel, put your hope in the LORD
both now and forevermore.

PSALM 131

I discovered some time ago that I am what educators call a kinesthetic learner. While some others learn primarily from seeing or being told, I learn by doing. So, for me, even the simplest task amounts to on-the-job training, trial and error, and the constant hands-on exploration of the essential question: *How do I do it?*

As a kinesthetic learner, I have particular trouble in the area of philosophical truth. I am the voice heard over and over again in the Bible—and sadly, often in the whining and suspicious tones of the Pharisee and the doubter—asking: Who *is* my neighbor? How *can* I be born again when I'm old? How can I believe unless

I put my fingers where the nails were and thrust my hand into his side? What good thing must I do before I can rest forever?

At 5:00 this morning, hardly able to tear my mind away from my morning to-do list (actually last week's list that never got done) to read the Bible and talk to God, my question was about giving my stress to the Lord. Easily said, I told the Bible reading part of myself crankily, but how exactly does one *do* that? Why doesn't the Lord just take it from me?

I was in Luke, where the terrified disciples woke Jesus to calm the storm. "Master, Master," they shrieked, "we're going to drown!" Implicit in their frenzy was a pointed question: "How can you be sleeping? Why are you doing nothing to help us?" I knew precisely how they felt.

As always, the question encapsulated its answer: Jesus "got up and rebuked the wind and the raging waters" and the disciples themselves.

"Where is your faith?" he asked them, and suddenly I realized that shrieking to Jesus to help me and having faith that he would take care of me were *not* the same thing. Faith, that elusive gift that I could not earn, did nevertheless require doing something, something specific. I had to calm myself with the certainty that I was loved and would be taken care of. "Like a weaned child with its mother," I had to calm myself enough to let my master sleep.

"Calm down," I used to tell my little daughters when they were unreasonably upset or over tired. I reminded them that I was in charge but that I knew they had the power to calm themselves. I made them sit on my lap and take deep breaths. I stroked their hair. After awhile, their tight little rebellious bodies would soften and lean into me.

Think of it! Jesus slept in that little boat while the dangerous storm raged. Giving my problems to Jesus is to let him sleep—and to sleep myself.

The Psalmist knew this: it is in vain, he tells us in Psalm 127, that we "rise early and stay up late, toiling for food to eat"—for the Lord "grants sleep to those he loves."

Relevant and cited scriptural passages: Psalm 127 and 131, Matthew 19:16–30, and Luke 8:22–25.

31

On Returning the First Essays of the Semester

I will praise the LORD, who counsels me;
even at night my heart instructs me.

Psalm 16:7

Last night I woke up and lay awake for hours, unable to fall back asleep. I had been suffering from a cold for the past few days, a bad one, and upon awakening made the delicious discovery that the congestion in my nose and chest and the irritating tickle in my throat were gone. Partly it was the air itself that delighted me: finally able to get through all the mucous, it was fragrant from the night and felt like warm ice moving through my sinuses and bronchial tubes. Partly, though, it was the pleasure of discovering that God had once again been listening to my little babbled prayers. *Let me get over this cold. Take it away from me. Make me well.*

Florence Nightingale, who, in addition to being the famous mother of modern nursing wrote voluminously on her Christian faith, once noted—with some smugness, I think—that true mystics never said prayers of petition. But I do. There's no pleasure like daring to ask and being given.

Indeed, I was so enthralled by these gifts—the sweet air, the gratitude—that I should have fallen straight back to sleep, but somehow I got to worrying about my English 101 students. I had given back their diagnostic essays the day before. I go to great lengths to be especially fair and lucid in my response to this first sample of their writing and give them a 100% on it, regardless of the state of their writing at the start of my course. Nevertheless, upon reading my comments and seeing the grade they would have gotten had this not been a diagnostic essay, they had changed in an instant from liking me and finding me funny to hating my guts.

Every semester, at this time, I reconsider this whole business of grading papers. On the one hand, despite all the scholarship to the contrary that one of my colleagues says proves that students never read what teachers write on their papers, I'm certain that the only way for them to improve their writing is to get an honest response. *This doesn't make sense*, I scribble in their margins. *You sound pompous. You're boring me.*

On the other hand, though, every studiously dropped face and angry thrust of the shoulder when I squeeze by to read my handwriting on someone else's paper cries out discouragement, and I am stricken. *Lift them up*, I hear those New Testament sages exhorting me, and for weeks after returning that first set of papers I am weighed down by guilt and an overwhelming consciousness of my own meanness.

Don't get me wrong. I heard those voices as I graded, too, and as I made my syllabi and planned my classes and argued once again, at our last department meeting before the new semester, in favor of students being held strictly accountable for usage and form in their writing as well as critical thinking. But—*lift them up,* the voices told me. *Encourage them. Nudge them gently forward.* And I took care to make positive remarks on their papers and begin each summary assessment with praise of what was good about the essay before going on to detail where work was needed.

But they don't seem to notice my encouraging remarks at all. Comically, these tend to be the comments they find hardest to read, and when I bend to decipher, they never look pleased to find out it said *Dynamite!* or *Great point!* One student yesterday even thought I was being sarcastic.

So, deep in the night, my sleep-blessed husband enjoying the night air beside me, I pondered my students' outrage and my meanness. *Am I wrong to grade so hard? Is there no other way? Why do I care so much if they like me?* I reminded myself in vain that most of them would quickly progress and eventually like me again, but it was those angry ones who wouldn't—who would steadfastly refuse to progress, who would steadfastly refuse even to put a comma before a coordinating conjunction joining two sentences and as steadfastly continue to despise me—that kept me awake. *How could I grow them as writers without acknowledging their areas of weakness? How could I be honest without hurting them?* I lay hating myself, my power to hurt, my ineptness in encouraging, my crazed desire to make writers of them, every one.

Some of my friends would call my night worries spiritual warfare, but I know God loves me and promises me the sleep I need. In fact, I eventually fell asleep and woke up more refreshed than I have felt in many days. My cold was gone, my daughters were in a good mood, and, even though the skim milk I always have on my cereal had gone sour, I felt excited about the day before me and calm.

And so, it seems, God has been counseling me in the night,

telling me what he knows as a parent and has told me time and again with respect to my own children: Stand firm in love.

"Like me," he says, "you will suffer their anger, and they will see your teaching as a desire to punish, your truth as an affront. Daily they will ignore your mercies and your encouraging words. They will, in short, hate the open hand you extend to them, and you, like me, will love long in vain, suffering sometimes years, sometimes a lifetime of disdain, before their names are but entries in some forgotten grade book."

I thought of my youngest, Lulu, when I correct her or do anything she doesn't like. She gets so angry she won't talk to me. In babyhood she made pronouncements like, "I don't even love you as much as half a sneakbug," which was a made-up creature of microscopic size.

Not long ago, when I accidentally put her smelly sneakers in the wash right before she left for soccer, she told me in her rage, "Mama, I will not let you come to soccer practice with me ever again."

As if I'm dying to go sit with a bunch of women I don't know and watch a bunch of children practice moves that make no sense to me, I thought of retorting.

And yet, her words cut me, and I said a little prayer that this disaster wouldn't ruin her practice and her evening with her dad, who is the assistant coach. And then, hours later, she returns home proudly wearing a pair of out-grown, hand-me-down cleats that someone happened to bring along to give away, just her size, and Big Sister doesn't even have cleats, which makes them even more precious, and she made a goal at practice, and she's so excited she climbs up into my lap to love on me, forgetting all her promised punishments.

God is so amazingly generous. I ask, he gives. Just like that. I worry; he counsels me in the night. He molds my very heart in his hands and instructs me in his ways.

Relevant and cited scriptural passages: Psalms 16, 127, and 139.

Other references:

Florence Nightingale. "Notes for Devotional Authors of the Middle Age: Collected, Chosen, and Freely Translated by Florence Nightingale." *Collected Works*, Vol. 4. Waterloo: Wilfrid Laurier UP, 2003.

32

Students in the Garden

The other day a passage in Acts sent me back to the end of the book of Amos to a passage that suddenly lit up for me and seemed to be an encapsulation of what the whole of scripture is about. I had been considering the question, all summer, of why Christians study. What should be different about the way students learn, the way I teach, in Christian academia? I had attended an intensive, two week long workshop at my university on the integration of faith and learning followed by a series of sessions on how to be a spiritual mentor to my students. I had been struggling, more specifically, with the spiritual relevance of what I teach as I put together my syllabi and designed the assignments and projects and even conversations I wanted to have with my students in the upcoming semester.

Even more specifically, I had before me my yearly problem course when it comes to spiritual relevance: Advanced English Grammar, a class more content intensive than my usual writing and literature courses and addressing a subject considerably less liked by my students and, for many, harder to do. Grammar is a subject about which I would inevitably be asked at some time during the semester, "What's the point of all this?" For the faith and learning workshop, I wrote a paper on my plan for integrating faith and grammar this semester, and I thought I had it licked.

Then I read Amos 9:13–15:

"The days are coming," declares the LORD,
"when the reaper will be overtaken by the plowman
and the planter by the one treading grapes.
New wine will drip from the mountains
and flow from all the hills.
I will bring back my exiled people Israel;
they will rebuild the ruined cities and live in them.
They will plant vineyards and drink their wine;
they will make gardens and eat their fruit.
I will plant Israel in their own land,
never again to be uprooted from the land I have given them,"
says the LORD your God.

It's a rich passage of reversals and promises and busy images of ruined cities under construction and all manner of farming going on and exiles coming home. It took me a minute or two just to figure out what I was seeing, what I was being told. But, even before I had it figured out, I knew at once that it held the answer to a summer's worth, perhaps a lifetime's worth, of questions.

Let me tell you what I saw. A field full of activity. Here a combine hard at work reaping corn, there a tractor pulling up the soft earth from under the stalks for the next harvest, here a woman carefully settling a young grape vine in the soil, and there workers gathering the ripe fruit in their baskets. Everyone getting in one another's way, always having to stop and laugh, eating bread and fruit and drinking wine and exchanging jokes and stories as they worked.

I have been in the field with tractors before. Plowing frantically before the rain arrived and making the dirt too wet to get through. Raking hay in front of my husband on the baler, anxious to finish baling the hay we had down before the sun fell away and the humidity went up and the grass that we had put so much work into cutting and drying and raking became too damp to bale. The longer it took to bale, the more nutrients would be leached out by the inevitable rain and dew. Once baled, the hay would smell moldy and cattle would find it less appetizing. We worked with these eventualities in mind, and they tightened even the best work day with worry.

Amos's vision was nothing like our single-minded toil. His was a crazy scene—everyone at cross purposes and not caring about deadlines or getting done. The work was a party. This, I thought—as the Jews have always thought in regarding this passage as Messianic—is what paradise will be like, when we return to our true home, never again to be uprooted from the land our Father has given us. It was a comfortingly chaotic and joyous picture, wholly unlike how I had imagined heaven before. Here were people going about their work and having fun, not worried about the outcome of their effort at all because they were enjoying, even as they worked, its amazing benefits: good food and wine, stories, humor, the company of friends. No one was stressed out. They seemed, in fact, to be having fun.

As usual when I get excited about something, I had to tell it to someone else, and it just happened to be that I told my daughters this time. And as usual whenever I try to teach them anything, I learned even more about the promises in those words as I spoke.

Lulu and Charlotte looked glaze-eyed when I read the passage from Amos, so I explained some of the words outside their usual vocabularies—words like *reaper* and *exiled* and *treading grapes*—and I had to go over as well the whole notion of biblical symbolism.

"Israel means God's chosen people," I told them. "That means the Israelites, but that also means us, because God chose us through Jesus. The Israelites' own land means Canaan, the land God picked out for the Israelites, but it also means Paradise, or Eden, the place God picked out for us, the earth as it used to be before the fall and how it will be again."

"This is how it was supposed to be," I summarized. "We, like Adam and Eve, were made to work and have fun and eat all at the same time." I thought of a photograph I have of Charlotte and Lulu in their Mamaw's garden as toddlers, wearing rubber work boots with their summer dresses, eating cucumbers among the leaves. I told them that this passage was God's promise that we would be like Adam and Eve in the garden again.

And even as I explained this I began to understand it—that Adam and Eve, in the garden, worked and played and ate fruit simultaneously, and that sin, in effect, separated the work from the product. After the curse, instead of enjoying our work, we labored. We worked in isolation from any satisfying results of our work, and we were buffered against the joy of labor by our preoccupation with all the dire occurrences—possible drought, an unwelcome rain, the night, the dew—that might prevent us ever seeing the products of our labor. That is what it means to toil, I think: to work in fear that we will lose what we are working for or never get done.

Sometime during the faith-and-learning workshop, I woke up with a song in my head from way back in my past. I played the tenor banjo as a teenager, and my teachers were always old men who played the songs of the old men who had taught them, so the music I learned to play was the music of the early twentieth century: a mixture of ragtime and Dixieland and silly croon tunes on flaky yellow sheet music that smelled like celery and cigarette smoke. The song, as I remembered it, went like this:

> Dear one,
> the world
> is waiting for the sunrise;
> every heart
> is heavy
> with dew . . .

That's all I remembered, and I wasn't even sure I remembered the song correctly, but those words and their halting tune kept going through my mind for a whole day. I didn't know why I was given this blip from twenty years behind me out of the blue, and, although I was discussing much more important things in my workshop, every once in a while I pondered the words. Why were their hearts heavy, I wondered, when dew, in songs at least, is usually thought of as a good thing? Is it not that we see as negative anything that interferes with the accomplishment of our toil or the fulfillment of our desires? So dew and rain, which my husband and I normally long for, are our enemies in the hayfield, and we hate both drought and rain when we are plowing. We can't appreciate the amazing abundance of God's gifts because we are so caught up in the task at hand, in getting it done.

"The mass of men," says Thoreau in *Walden*, "lead lives of quiet desperation." He envisions us "creeping down the road of life, pushing before [us] a barn seventy-five feet by forty, its Augean stables never cleansed, and one hundred acres of land, tillage, pasture, and wood-lot." We are, he says, "determined not to live by faith if we can avoid it."

Why should our waiting hearts be heavy with dew? I wondered now, reading the Amos passage anew. *Isn't the promise of restoration—making our gardens and eating our fruit—already fulfilled for us now as Christians? Has the Messiah not come? Is his Spirit not here with us already? Have we not been brought out of our exile to a home from which we can never be uprooted?*

I used to study Chinese, but back before I even started I met an elderly Russian man, a professor at the University in Shandung, who had spent his adult life in China. He had married a Chinese woman and raised a daughter who was my friend and suffered horribly during the Cultural Revolution. I must have been thinking about going into sinology even then, because I remember him warning me that the study of Chinese was a fruitless task. After a lifetime of Chinese, I'd be able to speak it fluently perhaps but would probably still struggle to read the newspaper, much less the Chinese classics. Studying Chinese, he told me, would be a waste of effort.

Later, as I progressed through the sinology program at the Freie University in Berlin and then at the Chinese University of Hong Kong, I found his words rang true. After years of study, I still struggled to make out the written language character by character. My reading was stilted and slow, and my mostly Japanese classmates in Hong Kong made fun of my handwriting. Beauty in writing was something Asian writers strove for, and I labored to make my characters look less ungainly. I remember writing out long reports on the topography of the United States and the history of the women's movement. I used Chinese onion skin writing paper that looked like graph paper, carefully centering one character per square. My professors and classmates invariably laughed at how the subject matter of my compositions didn't match my childish characters.

There was one thing that was not true about what that sad, hardened, hopeless Russian professor told me, and it was this: He neglected to mention—perhaps he didn't know—how much fun it would be to study Chinese words, to learn what each part of a character meant, that each assemblage of seemingly random strokes and dots represented a system and a history, a predictable way that the character should be made and almost invariably a divergence from that path, an abbreviation of some part of it or a pretty addition that made the character a puzzle, and that it would be fun to solve each one. I sat on the bed in my musty, hot little Hong Kong room and worked through puzzle after puzzle, then puzzled through how the characters all fit together in a sentence that made sense. Although I was accustomed to reading in other foreign languages, Chinese transformed the reading process for me. Each time I figured out a word or a sentence, I felt like a hero.

I had to look up most words in my Chinese-English dictionary, which was published in the People's Republic and defined everything in political terms. Once, when I read one of my compositions aloud in class, my professor—an exile from the People's Republic—asked me what I meant when I read the Chinese word for bitter melon, *kǔ-guā*. "*Kǔ*?" he kept asking, not understanding the word for *bitter*, and I finally made him understand by offering an example like the ones in my dictionary: "*Kǔ*!" I said, "You know, *Rénmín de shēnghuó hěn kǔ!*—The life of the people is very bitter!" He laughed in surprise. Studying Chinese, though of little use to me then and even less later, was nevertheless sheer joy.

What will paradise be like? We have what the Israelites yearned for, if we only knew it. In Christ, although we are surrounded by sin, in a real sense we are living in the garden. In him, our work *is* our fruit, and our enjoyment of it is the product of our labor. We were made to sow and reap, plant and tread grapes, eat and drink wine and have fun, simultaneously, and we could be doing that this very moment, if we only knew it. If we're not still waiting for the sun to rise, for our Messiah to arrive and fulfill scripture's promises, we should have all our heavy equipment out in the field at the same time. As Christians, knowing our purpose and our end, determined to live by faith, we can study this world with mad chaotic abandon.

Relevant and cited scriptural passages: Amos 9:13–15.

Other references:

Ernest Seitz and Eugene Lockhart. "Dear One, the World Is Waiting for the Sunrise." 1919.

Henry David Thoreau. *Walden; or, Life in the Woods.* 1854.

The Pinyin Chinese-English Dictionary. Wu Jingrong, ed. Beijing: Commercial, 1979.

33

At the Mountain

The LORD our God said to us at Horeb, "You have stayed long
enough at this mountain. Break camp and advance."
DEUTERONOMY 1:6–7

In the beginning of the Book of Deuteronomy, Moses recounts
to his people the story of the last few years: their struggles and
rebellions, his own burdens and worries, their wanderings and
hesitations. His voice whines and meanders, mixing in distant
events from a layered past as if they were recent and honing in on
a single theme: their indecision and resistance to change. "[Y]ou
were unwilling," he tells them. For "you did not trust in the LORD
your God" (1:32).

"'How can I bear your problems and your burdens and your disputes all by myself?'" (1:12) he remembers wondering and still won-
ders. He has apparently forgotten the moments in his own past when
he was beset by the same hesitation, the same indecision, the same
burdens and disputes within himself, when he told the God who
commanded him *but what if* and *I can't* and *I'm not cut out for this.*

"Because of you," Moses reminds the Israelites again and again,
"the LORD became angry with me" (1:37). "[B]ecause of you the
LORD . . . would not listen to me" (3:26). Because of you.

And throughout the narrative he seems unaware that he is speaking God's will to the people, God's answer to his own worries, the very words he reports that the Lord spoke to him at Horeb, in the desert, wherever he went: "That is enough . . . Do not speak to me anymore about this matter" (3:26). "You have stayed long enough at this mountain" (1:6).

If I listen to God when I am worried, I hear the same words. That's enough. Do not speak to me anymore about this matter. You have stayed long enough at this mountain. Move on.

Usually it's at night, and my worries are about my children and their rages, my students and their problems, my husband and his stress, my job and its exigencies. And if, in the darkness, I stop worrying to listen—which I often don't, or can't, or won't—I hear God's voice under the narrative of my own worries and accusations: That's enough. Do not speak to me anymore about this matter. You have stayed long enough at this mountain. Move on. Trust in me. Go to sleep.

Relevant and cited scriptural passages: Deuteronomy 1–3.

About the Author

P atty Kirk grew up in Southern California and the Connecticut countryside in a big Catholic family. Family traumas caused her to turn increasingly from her childhood faith during her teenage years. She pursued degrees in English at University of California at Irvine and Tulane University in New Orleans. In the wake of a crime of which she was the victim, she fled her home and spent the next ten years in Berlin, Beijing, and Hong Kong, searching for some sort of meaning or happiness or love or fulfillment that she never found in any of these places. During her years abroad, she studied various subjects—German, Anglo-Saxon, and Chinese at the Freie University in Berlin, Mandarin at the Chinese University of Hong Kong—and she taught English at colleges in Berlin, Beijing, and Hong Kong. She also wrote stories, hung out with friends, went to art museums, learned to cook what the people around her were eating, read. Finally, at thirty, she returned to the U.S. to study creative writing at the University of Arkansas, earning an MFA in fiction in 1991.

That same year, she married an Oklahoma farmer and settled

down to a life entirely unfamiliar to her. As if farming full time and country living were not strange enough, her husband was a Christian—not just the ordinary kind of Christian who goes to church and leaves it at that, but a genuine Bible Belt believer, who read the Bible every morning and prayed on his knees and regularly took the neighbor's son to the movies because, well, he was a neighbor. Nevertheless, three years and two children later, she became a Christian herself, and when cattle prices dropped in the mid-nineties, she went back to her old job of teaching, first at the local high school and then at a Christian university across the state line in Arkansas, where she still teaches.

God began infecting every aspect of her daily life, converting every struggle to a miracle and holding her to account for every apparent victory. She fought hard against these changes, in her marriage and parenting, her work, her mind. She recorded her battles with God in free-form spiritual writings part praise, part lament, part exegesis, woven together with narratives of her daily life and her sometimes unwilling research into what it means to believe in God.

Now she teaches, raises her daughters, and continues to write.

For additional information about Patty Kirk
and her books, go to www.amateurbeliever.com.

Acknowledgments

In this book, I depend for much of what I say on stories about friends and acquaintances who were instrumental in bringing me to the brink of faith and then, once I embraced God, nurturing my ongoing development as a believer. There are so many that I can't name them all here, but key among them are my sister Sharon and her husband Tom; the teachers of my first Bible study class, Monaray and Jamie Noah; and mentors at crucial points in my spiritual development, notably Mitzi Bingaman, Bonnie Osmon, and Susan Vila.

An entry into faith is a very private experience, comprising the most intimate details of a life, and, as a result, this is a very personal book. In it, I mention events and circumstances that many would not want even someone they loved to bring up in public. In some cases, I have changed names and blurred details or left them out entirely to make events less recognizable. But with my family such concealment was not possible. Some of them—especially my husband, my mother-in-law, and young daughters—have permitted their lives to be exposed through my ramblings, and for this I am especially grateful.

Others have helped me by encouraging me as a writer. Some, like my lifelong friend Carla Boyer, told me over and over again that I *was* a writer, which for some reason I keep needing to be told. Others read my work and said nice things. Chief among these are several of my students who worked closely with the book and have over the years become esteemed friends: Ali Arant, Ann Clipperton, Emily Culella, Ruth Hoffman, Lee Ella Oglesbee, and Leanna Ramsey. Fellow faith writer Kathleen Norris, although I only knew her for the space of a couple of days when she came to speak at my university, was as supportive in this regard as an old friend. She went out of her way to encourage me in my writing and even wrote a recommendation on my behalf. What a real person she is. What a Christian.

I always counsel my writing students that the best way to improve their writing is to read their work aloud, and I encourage them to nurture relationships that provide willing audiences. Such relationships are, in fact, rare. We have gotten out of the habit of being read to in modern times, and many these days cannot stomach it. So, to improve my own writing, I have had to resort to taking my audiences forcibly captive by announcing—to my husband, friends, unsuspecting colleagues alone in their offices and at meetings, fellow members of Fellowship Bible Church in Siloam Springs, the women of the John Brown University Women's Fellowship Book Club, and countless classes of restless students— that I was going to read to them what I had just written. It would have been rude to object, so they never did. Some of them obliged me further by attending my public readings. Every time I read aloud, in addition to learning what worked from my audience's laughter and remarks, I was also able to correct errors of cadence and style that I would otherwise have missed. Especially longsuffering listeners, in addition to those already mentioned as encouraging me in my writing, include my mother-in-law and my colleagues Don Balla, Cary Balzer, Li Ping and Frank Blume, Lisa Brandom, David Brisben, Carli Conklin, Tim Dinger, Gary Guinn, Jonathan Himes, Charles Pastoor, Cal Piston, Don Siemens, and David Vila.

I have been writing for a long time, but the exigencies of getting my writing published—constructing book proposals, researching *Publisher's Market*, making copies, going to the post office, filling out self-addressed stamped envelopes for the rejection letters, getting rejected, starting all over again—have loomed in my consciousness to the point at which I could barely motivate myself to do it. About once a year I sent out an essay to a journal, and it just about did me in. What a blessing, when I finally decided to send out the present book, to find a competent agent, Greg Johnson, to advocate on my behalf and take most of these matters out of my hands.

The people at Thomas Nelson have also been supportive and kind. They begin every interaction with accolades and teach me, by example, how I ought to interact with my own students. All told, the business of getting published has not been near as harrowing as I expected.

And then, of course, there's God, from whom all good things come. I thank him for inspiring my thoughts and enduring my speculations. None of my endeavors would be possible without his enthusiasm for the halting steps into his outspread arms that constitute this book.